Getting to Commitment

Getting to Commitment

Overcoming the 8 Greatest Obstacles to Lasting Connection
(And Finding the Courage to Love)

Steven Carter
with Julia Sokol

M. EVANS
Lanham • New York • Boulder • Toronto • Oxford

Published by M. Evans
An imprint of The Rowman & Littlefield Publishing Group, Inc.
4501 Forbes Boulevard, Suite 200, Lanham, Maryland 20706

Distributed by NATIONAL BOOK NETWORK

Library of Congress Cataloging-in-Publication Data

Carter, Steven, 1956–
    Getting to commitment : overcoming the eight
greatest obstacles to lasting connection and finding the
courage to love / Steven Carter with Julia Sokol
        p.   cm.
    ISBN 0-87131-889-5 (cloth)
    ISBN 0-87131-905-5 (paper)
    1. Man-woman relationships. 2. Interpersonal relations.
3. Commitment (Psychology)   I. Sokol, Julia. II. Title.
HQ801.C2885   1998
158'.2—dc21   98-22533

Design and typeset by Annemarie Redmond

Manufactured in the United States of America

To my wife, Jill, with love.

Acknowledgements

Every book happens because many people, in addition to the author(s) help make it happen, and this book is no exception.

First I must thank my wife Jill, who has been the inspiration for this book. Without her belief in love and the importance of a committed relationship, none of this would have been possible.

Next, unending thanks go to Julia Sokol, my long-term writing partner and 'co-expert', whose keen insights, understanding, and, outstanding literary talents shine through every project we work on together.

Thanks also to the many men and women who so generously shared their time and their stories with us so that others might benefit.

When I am searching for validation, for verification, and for greater insight into relationship issues, it gives me great comfort to know that I can turn to Dr. Irene Harwood. For the last seven years she has helped shape all my work, and I wish to thank her here.

And then there are many special little fuzzy creatures—Maggie, Carla, Holly, Harry, and Huck—who have their own special lessons to teach about love and commitment. God bless each and every one of you.

As always, my thanks to Barbara Lowenstein and her talented, committed staff for the work they are always doing behind the scenes.

Finally, I must give very special thanks to the staff at M. Evans publishing, and particularly to George de Kay for his intelligence and support these many years.

Contents

INTRODUCTION

Let's not be embarrassed about admitting who we are. We are the men and women whose relationships (or even marriages) never seem to work out. We fall in love, but we don't seem to be able to stay in love. Sometimes it's because the people we want are unable to love us back in the same way, and we are then left with broken hearts and destroyed dreams. Sometimes it's because we are the ones who fall out of love; then we are the guilt-ridden rejectors instead of the disappointed rejectees. Either way, typically we once again begin the search for new partners, hoping against hope that the next one will be the "right one." More than a few of us have had our hopes dashed so many times that all we want to do is sit home with our computers, television sets, CD players, or our loving cats and dogs.

Our parents look at us, and they wonder, what's wrong. Our happily married friends try to introduce us to appropriate mates, even as they wonder, what's wrong. We spend evenings with equally unattached single friends, and together we wonder, what's wrong. They write sit-coms about people like us, but it looks a lot more fun on the small screen than it feels in real life.

Here's the problem: Many of us are starving for a loving and committed connection to another person. Even so we sabotage and undermine our chances at finding the love we want. In the most simple language, we don't understand commitment; we don't know how to make and keep the connections that matter most. As we form relationships, we discover that it's difficult to be vulnerable; it's difficult to feel trust. It's difficult to make good choices and it's difficult to find what we think we want. It's difficult to open our hearts.

As much as we may protest that we seek genuine relationship, too often we are more attracted to fantasies than to real people. And frequently we also want unrealistic guarantees. We want to know what the future will hold; we want to know for sure that both we and the partners we choose will be able to deliver on our initial promises. A fact of life, however, is that real love offers no guarantees. We are not always perfect, those we love are not always perfect, and the unions we form are not always perfect.

Once upon a time, whenever two people said "I love you" to each other, whenever two people had sex together, whenever two people shared common space, they were together for life. Not so anymore. These days we live in a world that seems to value change more than anything else. We get up in the morning, pick up our newspapers, turn on our computers, and immediately start searching for things that are new and different. "What's next" and "how soon will it get here" seem to be our rallying cries. Our society frequently values individuality more than partnership, freedom more than connection, and perfectionist standards more than compromise. And our relationships are mirroring these trends. There are so many options, so many possibilities, so many choices. It's easy to believe that relationships can be as disposable, replaceable, and upgradeable as everything else.

Given the tenor of the times, it's clear to see why some of us are nervous about how much we should be investing in the future of relationships in general or one relationship in particular. We behave accordingly. In our personal lives, too often we find ourselves creating distance between ourselves and our partners. We construct extraordinary barriers and create complicated situations so that we will never be truly vulnerable. The reasons why we do this are fairly obvious: To commit ourselves to the act of loving means that we are committing ourselves to a potentially risky situation in which our tender hearts might be hurt. And, of course, to commit to another person also brings with it another kind of risk: Getting stuck in a relationship that we might later regret.

Yet, as many of us have discovered, running away from love always brings us back to the same old place. That's also frightening. We ask ourselves: What will happen if we are not capable of making a genuine loving commitment? Will we be living the kinds of lives we say we want? This question reflects one of the great conundrums of human existence. To love another is to be exposed to the possibility of all the complicated stuff—messy as well as wonderful—that can happen between two people. To be alone and lead an uncommitted life is . . . well, to be alone and live an uncommitted life. There are certainly arguments that can be made for both states. But if you want love and human connection, be prepared to take some risks.

There is one important note I want to make here before I continue. Commitment fears and commitment struggles are universal problems that are neither a product of, nor the sole domain of any one sexual orientation. Though I often use he/she language and examples in the pages that follow, these are not exclusively heterosexual issues. These are human issues.

Love is always going to present us with challenges. For some people these challenges will be viewed as insurmountable obstacles. But others realistically look at the very same challenges and see them as opportunities to grow and to stretch. Falling in love and staying in love requires it's own kind of heroism. If we are to experience intimacy, our hearts have to be brave as well as loving. That's because it takes real courage to love; it take real courage to make a commitment. This book is about finding that courage.

Love Is a Process,
Not a Solution

I'm standing in front of a small audience of very well intentioned women, and men, who are investing their time, their money, and their hopes to attend a lecture on commitment and commitment conflicts. As always I have asked members of the audience to write down three questions that they would hope to have answered before the end of the evening. While they are signing in, I look at the questions. I do this carefully even though I probably already know them by heart. As much as I appreciate that each question reflects the unique personality and dilemma of the individual questioner, the truth is that the questions I'm asked are always fundamentally the same.

"How can I deal with a partner who is afraid to commit . . . a partner who doesn't let me get close . . . a partner who avoids intimacy?"

"Why do I get scared in relationships?"

"How do I know whether I'm afraid of commitment in general, or just this specific relationship?"

"I keep choosing people who are afraid of commitment. What does this say about me?"

"What can I do to help a partner who says he/she is scared?"

"One of us always seems to be afraid of moving forward. How can we break this pattern?"

Every time I schedule one of these talks and look at these questions, I wonder what I can say to make a difference to these people. I know what kind of disappointment and pain brings a person to one of these lectures. I know how hard it is to expose one's personal life to a group of strangers. I know how much work goes into having a good relationship. What I don't know is whether people are prepared to do the work that is required. I know for sure that fast answers are simply not enough. There are no quick fixes.

Sometimes as I stand in front of these men and women, I want to say, "Even if I share everything I know as honestly and openly as possible, are you really sure you want to know what I know? Will that help you? Because if you are sincere, then you have a problem: You will have to do something with this new information. You will have to change the way you think and act. You will have to do something differently in your relationship with yourself as well as your relationships with others. This takes time and work, and it isn't always pleasant."

During the nineties, many of us got into the habit of watching *Seinfeld*. Each week, we looked at George Costanza, and we laughed at the consistency of his problems. One thing we could count on was that George was not going to change. I remember one episode in particular: George fell in love with a woman in prison; her situation made her the ultimate in unavailable partners. How typical! By definition the relationship was limited and would put few demands on George. Of course, he was enthralled. And, of course the relationship fell apart as soon as the woman got out of jail. As always nothing changed. We can laugh at George, but often our behavior is just as predictable. In our relationships, we follow the same patterns time and time again. We either make the wrong choices or we mess up potentially good relationships. But in real life, it's just not funny. We can laugh through our tears, but the tears are still there. I believe there is little that feels more empty and painful than being incapable of forging a working commitment with another person. It implies a lifetime of missed opportunities, first dates, and failed connections. How dissatisfying.

The message is that for most of us, the "eyes-closed thing" isn't working any more. We keep bumping into the same objects and ending up in the same dark places. All we have to show for our efforts are the bumps and bruises that come from repeatedly hitting the familiar walls and experiencing the same negative emotions. If old patterns haven't worked in the past, what makes us think they will work in the future? They didn't get us into the open spaces of relationships; they didn't help us find the love we want.

Ten years ago, I knew everything there was to know about *not* making a commitment. I knew everything about romantic fear—every nuance, every gesture, all of the language and all of the behavior. I was an expert, if not *the* expert on fear. A thousand and one different ways to run away from love. For a while in my life, running away from love had

for most of us, the "eyes-closed thing" isn't working

it's own appeal; sometimes it was even fun. Fun to be ducking, dodging, and dating. Then it became awful. I wanted long-term love. I wanted a real life. I wanted to be able to share a deep commitment with another human being. I wanted to be able to fall in love and stay in love. I wanted to be able to make a real commitment.

Some people may honestly believe that they can live very happy lives without having a stable relationship. They say commitment is not an essential ingredient in their lives; they say this is not how everybody wants to live. I agree. Not everybody does. But it's how *I* wanted to live, and if you have picked up this book, a committed relationship must certainly be something that you desire. Now, you probably want to know how you can get from that place of desire to a place where you have the relationship you want.

My job is to help you get down the road. My job is to demystify the process, familiarize you with your options and tell you about the common pitfalls so you don't veer too far off the path. The tough stuff is up to you. There is only one difference between those who make it through and those who do not. One single difference, and it has nothing to do with your age, history, or desire. The one single difference is courage.

Examining My Own Fear of Commitment

One hot summer day more than ten years ago, I found myself in Chicago, sitting on stage at the *Oprah Winfrey Show,* waiting for the cameras to start rolling tape again after the commercial break. The subject of the show was "commitmentphobia."

The show was going out live to much of the country, and for the first thirty minutes, several men sat on stage and spilled their insides to an audience of riveted viewers. It gave the appearance of an on-air confession, and it was coming from a group of normal looking guys who were acknowledging their problems with romantic commitment and long-term love. Talking about their relationships and their problems with women, these men were taking responsibility for their share of broken promises, broken dreams, and broken hearts. The studio audience was surprisingly sympathetic. The women particularly seemed grateful for the honesty as well as appreciative for the new insight and understanding into a problem that had touched many of them personally.

Then it was my turn to talk. But I was not there to tell my story. I was there for a different reason. I was there because I had just published a book called *Men Who Can't Love.* In this book my co-author, Julia Sokol, and I coined the term *commitmentphobia* to describe people who have a claustrophobic response to inti-macy. This book, which offers a self-protective message for women involved with commitmentphobic men, is devoted to understanding this problem.

I remember that day vividly. On stage, with Oprah Winfrey in front of me asking her first question, I am terrified. I glance at Julia for assurance. She knows just how terrified I am. Not only because it's *Oprah,* but also because I have my own unpleasant little commitmentphobic secret that I would like to keep off the screen. Right now I am painfully aware that even though I am the show's "expert," I am no better than any of the men who have already spoken. In many ways, I am worse. I have never been in a committed relationship. The obvious questions I am dreading are very simple ones. "Mr. Carter, what about you?" "What about your life?" "What do you really know about intimacy?" "What about your relationships?" "What about your own commitment fears?"

Now, I want you to understand that I know that there are no rules that say that someone writing about relationships has to be living a perfect life. There are no rules that say I cannot be struggling with my own commitment issues. For years all kinds of experts have invoked the "do as I say, not as I do" clause to explain and justify their own behavior. To some extent, this is valid. Just because the messenger is flawed doesn't mean that the message isn't reliable. Ultimately for the messenger, however, this kind of reasoning is bound to wear thin. Besides, on that day, I was ashamed of the way I had behaved in many, if not all, of my relationships. So ashamed that I could not imagine telling my whole story to anyone, let alone millions of anyones—and on national television. As a relationship expert, my veneer of superiority was being severely tested, and it was humiliating.

After *Men Who Can't Love* was published, I received scores of mail from women who asked if I somehow knew their boyfriends, husbands, or lovers. How else, they wanted to know, could I have so uncannily detailed their relationships. One of the reasons why the book so accurately described the behavior of people with commitment issues is because I was one of those people. Yes, hundreds of other men and women were interviewed about their relationships, but even though the details were different, their stories were my stories. When it came to running away from love, there was little that I had not done, said, or felt. I had pursued all the "wrong" relationships, and run away from all the ones that had the potential to be "right."

Writing a book about commitment fears had helped me. Some. But not enough. It had made me see very clearly how my behavior was hurting women. It had made me acutely aware that my ambivalence and, let's face it, cowardice, had created pain as well as confusion. Once the book was published, I felt as though I had been completely busted. I could no longer justify my old ways of being in relationships. I had to do something new. But what?

Some people run away from love by pursuing partners who are on the run

I figured that if I didn't do any of the things I wrote about, somehow my romantic relationships would change. Researching and writing about commitment problems made it impossible for me to go back to my old patterns. So what I did was shift gears into something far more dangerous—for me. For years I had been an active commitmentphobic, running away from women who acted as though they wanted me. I was too guilty and aware to do that anymore. But what could I do instead? My foolish knee-jerk reaction was fairly classic. I began to run away from love by pursuing women who were themselves on the run. Deeply ashamed of my inability to commit, I formed some new excuses for myself by somehow finding women who were themselves hard-pressed to commit to a date, let alone a long-term relationship.

Soon after *Men Who Can't Love* was published I started dating a woman who could turn on a dime. My head was spinning from this relationship. I think I knew I wasn't in love, but I was certainly in a fair amount of pain. I was getting a first-class education in what it meant to want someone who doesn't really want you—at least not for very long.

The week that *Men Who Can't Love* hit the bestseller list, my phone was ringing off the hook. Some of these calls were from people congratulating me, but there were also a fair number of friends as well as a couple of ex-girlfriends who called to say that they were finally beginning to understand *my* behavior. My current girlfriend, in the meantime, wasn't sure whether or not she could commit herself to meeting me for dinner. The relationship was making her feel a little pressured. Maybe next week? Suddenly I began to *really* understand the pain of women involved with men who forge and break connections. In the meantime I had a publisher who wanted a new book, one that would take up where *Men Who Can't Love* had left off, and I had a mailbox that was crammed full of letters from people asking me how to break commitmentphobic patterns. They wanted to know how to move forward. So did I. But I didn't know how.

The truth is that *Men Who Can't Love* gave, and gives, readers much needed insight. It gives information, perspective, and many self-protective guidelines. These are all very important things. I was, and am, very proud of the book. To this day, I think it remains one of the most honest and comprehensive examinations of commitment issues. But as much as I could describe, analyze, and even predict the patterns of men and women who run away from love, I didn't know what to do to change it. Not in my own life, and not in theirs.

Today I think I do.

Forming Intimate Connections

When we talk about love and commitment what we are really talking about is the capacity to handle the connections in our lives. Everything we do in life is about connecting. Connecting to our friends, work, homes, children, pets, communities, and even our planet. Good connections help us feel joy and happiness; bad connections can make us feel miserable and angry. The absence of meaningful connections can lead to emptiness and despair.

When we are connected to someone (or something) else, we are present and available. Typically a romantic relationship is defined by the degree to which the partners are bonded or connected—the degree to which they are present and available for each other. When we make a commitment to another person we are agreeing to be present and available; we are announcing that it is our sincere intention to stay connected.

Relationships survive or fail according to the level and integrity of the connectedness between the two partners. When a relationship is tested, it is the connectedness—the bond—that is put to the test. A lack of deep connection, complex connection, meaningful connection, and the relationship is likely to fail the test.

When we talk about connection, we also have to talk about disconnection—and the capacity to handle separation. For when it comes to your relationships, how you handle separation is often every bit as telling and meaningful as how you handle intimacy.

I know a woman who put on about twenty pounds in the first five months of a new relationship. Every single night after her new partner left her house, she found herself eating big bowls of comfort food—pudding and/or buttered noodles. She told me she was completely out of control. When she was with him, she felt "fine," but if he left her house in the evening, there she was in the kitchen, stirring up a storm. She never did this when she didn't have a relationship. It's not that she can't be alone. She has always done just fine alone. But once she connects to someone, she is reduced to a quivering, primitive mass of pudding-eating fear. Every time he leaves, it feels traumatic. This woman had the wisdom to understand that this response had nothing to do with her partner. He was doing nothing intentional to trigger her anxiety. She has a history of trauma associated with separations, and she brings this history into every relationship.

With the people we love, we always have to survive a never-ending process of connecting and disconnecting. In relationships, we come together, move apart, and then come together again. Monday morning arrives, and the couple who spent the idyllic weekend together is pulled apart by the real world. What will each of the partners be thinking and feeling when they are separated by their independent lives? When they said good-bye, both partners appeared to be completely attuned. Will the connection hold firm in their separate day-to-day worlds, or will one or both of them become so swept up in new experiences that what they shared will become weakened? Will the necessary period of disconnection be emotionally uneventful or will it be filled with intense anxiety, jealousy, or obsessive longing?

Men and women with commitment issues almost invariably experience serious difficulty handling connection and disconnection in an appropriate way. Often they attempt to shortcut the process or get around it entirely. Sometimes they form intimate bonds that seem as instantaneous as they are inappropriate. Other times, they erect enormous boundaries that keep their partners up in the air and prevent real bonds from forming.

Love Is a Process, Not a Solution

If I continue to repeat this sentence, it's because so many of us don't want to believe it. We grew up wanting—and expecting—love to be something magical that changes everything on its first visit, and changes it forever. We may have hoped to meet the perfect stranger. We grew up honestly believing that the experience of meeting that special someone and falling in love would transform the way we felt about ourselves and the world *PERMANENTLY*. We wanted to believe that love changes everything in the blink of an eye—magically and instantaneously. That is how we defined love. Often, even as we mature, we hang on to this unrealistic view of how people relate to each other.

My friend Mike, for example, is trying to decide whether or not to move in with a woman he has been dating for the past year. I asked Mike when he felt most deeply connected to his girlfriend. He answered that it was deepest when they first met. This made it clear to me that he has not moved on to that other level of relating where you look back at the beginning and see it as lovely, but also a little bit primitive. If he still thinks he had his most powerful connection in the beginning, then someone has clearly not let this relationship mature. Mike acknowledges that he is the partner who is resisting growth.

Years ago, a woman who was involved with a deeply commitmentphobic man told me that her therapist had once pointed out that this troubled relationship had never progressed past the first magical date. It always had all the passion and intensity of a charged first meeting, but it never developed to the point where anything could be taken for granted. Not even the next time they would meet. On one level that was very romantic and exciting. On another, it was hell.

Yes, a new romance feels magical. And yes, some of it feels instantaneous. But that's only the beginning of a loving relationship—the primer on a paint job that will have thousands of coats. Love is something that evolves in stages, changing as it grows. New lovers may think their connection is very strong. But it is only over time, if we are very lucky, that we can experience the full power of the extraordinary experience of genuinely loving another human being.

Creating an intimate connection means revealing yourself to this other person, who is your partner, through your actions, words, and feelings while, hopefully, he or she is doing the same thing in return. To create this kind of connection requires that both parties are able to get close and stay close long enough for a bond to form.

Think about the many ways we reinforce our connections to another person: Connections are formed through social contact and conversation; connections are formed through lovemaking; connections are formed through

Love is something that evolves in stages

shared experiences. We all know that intimate connections are deepened through shared emotions, vulnerabilities, and problems. Don't forget the connections that are created through doing nothing at all, but doing it together, like sitting in the living room, reading the paper or watching television without having to speak.

When we love someone, and want to increase our sense of connectedness, we try to do so by doing things together. We increase our knowledge and understanding of the other person by sharing our interests. We invite the people we love into our world to meet our friends and our families. This strengthens our connection.

As a relationship develops, all of these connections are happening at once, overlapping each other, as all kinds of bonds are being formed. These are the bonds that can withstand almost any kind of weather.

People who have difficulty with commitment typically don't let these ties develop naturally. More often than not, they are more connected to their fantasies than they are to another real, living, human being. Maggie, a woman who was involved in a long on-again, off-again relationship with a man who was resisting commitment, recently told me that it took her years to realize that many of her super-intense feelings were based on her connection to her dreams, not to a real person. If she had been able to look at her partner realistically, she would have seen and acknowledged the absence of true connections.

Commitmentphobic relationships are unions in which one or both partners are resisting commitment. Often the partner who is running away from love does so by constructing boundaries that keep connections from forming or deepening. These relationships may start out with almost instant intimacy and a strong sexual connection, but then one partner refuses to allow further connections to develop. Ultimately the relationship may become heavily lopsided. There are strong emotional bonds of passion and intensity, but the other ties of shared experiences are lacking. The relationship never opens up and grows.

Many times we think we have made a powerful connection only to realize later that the connection itself had no teeth. We may think we have experienced a special bonding only to see that the bond was a superficial one, or one based on false information or, worse, fantasies and false hopes.

We are sometimes so anxious to find love that we are seduced by the possibility of a loving connection long before a real connection is made. We often painfully discover that some people simply can't form real connections. They may do a great meeting, or a great phone call, or a great ten minutes. But they can't keep showing up. They can't be real and stay real. It all feels too vulnerable, too raw, too exposed. There are too many chances to get rejected, hurt, misunderstood, or manipulated.

If you make a genuine connection, you continue to tie little pieces of yourself to little pieces of someone else. Making a deep connection means tying thousands of these little pieces together over the course of time. It means watching some of these knots break, and it means retying new and stronger knots. That's why the fabric of each relationship is so unique and unusual.

At the beginning of a relationship, it makes sense to maintain some persona and interact with a little distance. When you are going to meet a stranger, it's not wise to bring and show everything you have. That would be dangerous and foolish. But if you are going to form a lasting and gratifying connection with another, ultimately all parts of you must be revealed—in stages of course. When we keep large chunks of ourselves disconnected from our partners, we end up dancing on the surface of our relationships. We end up with fragile bonds—fair weather bonds. These can feel good at times, but they lack the depth and richness to make us feel truly *and* permanently connected.

Men Who Can't Love was a book about understanding the commitment problem. This is a book about taking the necessary steps to get to commitment. I often meet women who say that they can now recognize a commitmentphobic man from across the room. At the first whiff of any singular symptom, the label gets attached and everything ends. It would be nice if it were always that clear cut, but it isn't. Most of us have the potential to be "runners." Most of us also have the potential to engage in successful relationships.

Today my life is very different than it was ten years ago. I am happily married to a stable, loving, and lovely woman. I want and expect to stay in the relationship I have. I'm happy with it. I don't feel as though I made any compromises I can't live with; I don't feel as though I have sold out. None of this is an accident. My wife jokes that I am the hardest working guy in the relationship business. She knows what she is talking about. I have worked very hard to get where I am. If I can reach this point, so can you.

Getting Beyond
the Eight Obstacles to Love

*T*here are some fundamental challenges standing between you and the relationship you deserve. These will almost inevitably be met every time you attempt a connection. They are not unique to you, or to your relationships. In fact, in many ways, they are archetypical and define relationship itself.

At the risk of being overly simplistic, I've narrowed these challenges down to eight very specific hurdles. Hah, you may be saying: Only eight! You may feel as though there are eight hundred or for that matter eight million. Some of you may feel so exhausted from your attempts to connect with another person that you may feel that no matter how many challenges there are, it is just too many. One too many hurdles to leap; one too many compromises to make. One too many lessons to learn; one too many hardships to overcome.

Many people have a chronic unwillingness to take on these relationship challenges. Often they have very deeply held fantasies about how effortless the right relationship should be. They believe that falling in love and staying in love should be completely effortless. Every time they hit a bump, they think something is wrong with their partners, themselves, or the match itself. This is a self-defeating attitude.

If you want to buy a new house or apartment, you know that there will be a series of obstacles that must be overcome. First you have to know that you have the downpayment. Then you need a realtor you can trust, one who will help you find the space that suits your needs. Once you find the space, you need a lawyer, and you have to go through the ordeal of getting various inspections, as well as securing a mortgage and an insurance policy. Finally if you are lucky enough to survive the various negotiations and the closing itself, and find yourself as the owner of this new home, the hard work has just begun. In a house you might have to worry about plumbing, heating, electricity. *The roof.* In a co-op, you have to worry about the board, and maintenance, maintenance, maintenance. The process is endless, time-consuming, financially debilitating, and a pain in the ass in so many ways. But the unique reward makes it all worthwhile. The same is true of relationships.

When we are looking for a place to live, we accept the fact that we must take certain steps. The process is nonnegotiable. If this is what you want, this is what you must do. Yet when it comes to relationships, often we still resist the notion of process and hard work. Sure, we might give the hard work of being with another person lip service, but when the struggle begins, in our heads we frequently start looking for a different solution—"maybe there is someone else . . . ," "maybe I would be better off single . . . ," "maybe I'm just not ready . . . ," "maybe I'm making a mistake."

When people describe the "hard work" of relationships, what they are almost inevitably describing is meeting one of these eight challenges. Trying to engage another human being means engaging this process. There are no shortcuts. We have to face these challenges. If we don't, we pay the price in the ways in which our relationships are limited.

Though we will be looking at these obstacles one-by-one, they don't necessarily present themselves separately this way "in the wild" as it were. In the process of relationship, you will be dealing with many of these, if not all, concurrently. On any given day, some will be more prominent than others, but these challenges don't represent eight stages. They are more like eight different directions from which resistance might come.

In my own experience I found it very important to identify and separate each of these. When you play divide and conquer this way, it gives you an edge. Taken all together, on the other hand, these challenges can become like one frightening mass or one insurmountable problem. I found that by separating out the principle elements and handling them piece by piece, these challenges became surmountable. I think you will too.

CHALLENGE ONE

The Courage to Stop Blaming

*B*eth's friends love her. That's probably why they are so sincerely worried about her. Her family is also concerned. They don't understand why a beautiful, talented woman like Beth can't find a man who appreciates her wonderful qualities. Beth wonders the same thing. She thinks a great deal about the men who failed her: Sam, the man whom she was sure she was going to marry until he told her he was marrying someone else; Eric, the man with whom she was sure she could develop a good relationship if only he would agree to see her more than once a month; Hank, the man with whom she shared passionate, loving sex even though he refused to share any part of his social life; Barry, the man who only wanted to share his social life and refused to have sex. What a list! Where did she find them? Why did she find them?

Beth still has feelings for some of these men. She has no real idea of what went wrong in any of these relationships. All she knows is what she feels: that the men in her life have ultimately rejected her. If asked why she doesn't have an ongoing loving relationship in her life, she would say it's because of the men she's known. She might even blame men in general. She doesn't seem fully able to realize that she had a part in choosing these men; she had a part in the outcome of these relationships.

Sam is one of the men Beth went out with. He's also single and lonely. Oh, he did get married, as he told Beth he would. But he was divorced within a year. If you ask Sam why none of his relationships have worked out, he has some fairly complicated explanations. He does feel that he loved Beth. They had a strong sexual bond. Nonetheless Sam decided that he couldn't marry Beth because he thought she was too dependent on her family. He also felt that Beth, who was a school teacher, didn't have an interesting enough career.

When Sam met the woman he did marry, he was quite smitten with her ambition, independent spirit, and outgoing personality. She had all the qualities Beth didn't. But she had a few negative qualities of her own. Sam ultimately found her rejective, demanding, and spoiled. In fact, Sam admits that he divorced his wife because she had few of the qualities Beth did. Sam had been married once before in his twenties, and although he likes many of the things marriage provides, both of his marriages were quite stormy and disturbing.

Sam now has a new relationship which he doesn't think will last because the woman "doesn't have good legs," and Sam, who is genuinely concerned about his capacity for fidelity, doesn't think he could stay married to someone unless she had a fabulous body.

Of course these brief descriptions of Beth's and Sam's personal histories are very simplistic and don't fully describe the emotional resonance. Beth, for example, has become more and more depressed with each of her break-ups. She has also become frightened of relationships in general. Like Sleeping Beauty, she keeps shrinking further back into her own shell, waiting and hoping for a Prince, who will appreciate her fine qualities and waken her with a kiss.

Unlike Beth, Sam is always out there searching for the right partner. He looks and looks. And he *always* discovers women he's attracted to. But no matter how strong the initial attraction, he finds each of them somehow flawed. There is one woman, for example, who he's been interested in for years, but she's married to someone else—a close friend, in fact. These days, Sam is so confused by his emotional ups and downs that his behavior is making him numb.

Beth and Sam have a great deal in common besides the fact that they went out together for a couple of years. They are both convinced—absolutely convinced—that the primary reasons why their relationships have failed revolve around their various partners' shortcomings. Beth wants a mate who will make her feel loved—whole and complete. Sam wants the same thing. They both think they are ready for "the real thing"; they both feel they are deserving of love. They both see themselves as being well-intentioned. Both believe they are loving. And both blame their partners for somehow not being "enough."

> **When our relationships go south, we all tend to want to blame our partners**

When our relationships go south, we all tend to want to blame our partners—their short-comings, their neuroses, their commitment issues. If I stop and think about this long enough—and if I am able to be honest enough—I know that I consistently blamed my partners for the failure of my relationships—even when I said I wasn't doing that.

I remember being in a relationship from which I was with-holding a full commitment. My partner was justifiably annoyed. The more politically correct part of me was telling her that this was my problem, not hers. In fact, we would often have long soul-searching conversations in which I would explain that I was the one who couldn't love fully. That I didn't even love myself fully. That I didn't even know myself. My partner acted as though she believed my words. But did *I*? Did I really? No.

Even as I was talking, another voice inside my head was thinking: *She* is the reason I can't move forward. She's the reason I can't feel more committed. She's not...something. And then I would go through all the ways in which she was a little bit less than perfect. Less than perfect for me; less than perfect in general. Never for a moment considering the countless ways in which *I* was less than perfect.

Not long after the relationship dissolved, this truly terrific woman and I took one of our final walks together. I still needed to justify the breakup because I was, not surprisingly, feeling quite defensive. My defensive position led to the most offensive conversation. I remember that I began this long insane ramble about how my brain was like a sophisticated mainframe computer while hers was like a home pc. While we were both equally intelligent (I lied because I didn't really believe that at the time) and ultimately both capable of accomplishing the same tasks (I didn't believe that either), I lived at a speed that was different from hers. I needed more input from more channels. I needed much more stimulation. I need to multi-task. Yes, I'm embarrassed to admit I actually said this. Why this woman didn't knee me in the groin and drop me in the sand right there I don't really know. Probably because she was a much smarter, much more decent, and much more human, human being than I was. Clearly I had lost my mind.

You can imagine how embarrassing it is for me to admit that this happened, especially to thousands of readers whose respect I have struggled for years to gain. But I need to share this story to make it painfully clear how crazy we can get in our own heads when we can't take responsibility for our own commitment conflicts.

STARTING RIGHT HERE, STARTING RIGHT NOW

Your first challenge on the path to commitment is to get a handle on all the ways you self-destruct in relationships. This is about how *you* do *yourself* in. This has nothing to do with what John, Jane, Bob or Barbara did, or didn't, do.

If you are picking potentially wonderful partners, and you are walking away from them because of your fears, you are responsible.

If you are getting involved with commitmentphobic partners and staying with them, you are still responsible.

Are you getting my drift here? The first challenge on the road to love is to have the courage to get a handle on your behavior and your romantic history. You can't keep looking outside of yourself for something that starts inside. Granted, you may have had some wildly difficult partners. But starting right now, you have to ask yourself, "How do I do this?" "What are my patterns?" "What are my excuses?" "What do I refuse to see?"

The only thing that will enable your eyes to open is the willingness to accept responsibility for your own commitment issues and how they play out. That is the "open sesame," the password to a different beginning.

Take My Word for It, Everybody Has *Some* Commitment Issues

The fact is that most of us have commitment conflicts. Some of us just handle them better than others. I don't know anybody who doesn't like the idea of a stable, loving relationship and a partner with whom to share romantic experiences. I also don't know anybody who doesn't like the idea of having all the intense new feelings as well as the lighthearted fun that a seriously exciting single life can provide. As we mature, hopefully we realize that we can't be home for the holidays with the kids and the partner and also be at the most glamorous singles resort in the Caribbean having sex for the first time with the best-looking date in the world.

Commitment conflict is normal. Even the most loving relationships demand hard work. Even in the best relationships we must relinquish certain freedoms (personal, financial, sexual) in exchange for a loving bond. You are *supposed* to have conflict. Part of the human condition is to experience this conflict. What is important is not the conflict itself, but how you *handle* it.

If you can't acknowledge your commitment issues, conflicts, and fears—whatever they may be—how can you do anything but handle them badly. The thing that worries me more than anything is talking to a man or woman who absolutely *insists* that he or she has no commitment fears. Sometimes this is a man who insists that if he met the "right" partner, he would be able to make a full commitment; sometimes this is a woman who is having a difficult time recovering from the end of a relationship with a man who ran away. Neither of them see their own patterns.

part of being human is being at least a little bit ambivalent about commitment

I firmly believe that any time your conflict is so completely underground, it is likely to be running the whole show. I know what I'm talking about. I ran from my own conflicts for many years, and they filled me with such shame that I did nothing but handle them badly. I judged myself negatively, tried to hide from my reality, and wound up continually screwing up my life. I could not face and handle my conflicts in a healthy way so they ended up handling me. They dictated my behavior, my choices, and my feelings.

Whether you are a "wild and crazy" single or a monogamous, devoted husband and father of three, part of being human is being at least a little bit ambivalent about commitment. Commitment *is* scary. No matter how much you love your partner, part of being human is having some fear and anxiety. It's normal. Working through these fears in the context of a stable relationship with a well-intentioned partner is a sign of emotional maturity.

I know that when I was experiencing my most extreme commitment issues, I found that I had two types of friends who in some ways personified both possible life styles. One group was like me—fellow runners—with whom I could talk about my relationship fantasies and failures; in the other group were friends who were completely connected to the world—people who were like anchors to me. This latter group were glued to the earth with children and mortgages and pets. These friends were kind enough to let me settle in their living rooms briefly in order to tell my sad stories. It was entertaining for them, and it was grounding for me. However, I could never stay there for very long. It was almost too calming. I know that they sometimes looked at me as though I was a creature from another world. They thought I was out of my mind for wanting such a stressful, disconnected life. Yet it was the only one I knew how to have.

I enjoyed visiting my romantically settled friends; however, I didn't really envy them. In fact, no matter how upset I might be, I often felt superior. Their love seemed cozy, but it also seemed "small." I was looking for something larger—an avalanche of feeling and power and connection and specialness. What, I wondered, did these people really know about love. Their problems seemed so mundane and day-to-day.

I've been interviewing men and women with commitment conflicts for years. I'm always struck by how contemptuous they can be of their committed brethren. As they look around at their friends and peers, all they seem to be able to see are people who they think have somehow "settled" for a less than perfect love. I know how they feel. They feel they are searching for a specialness that these other people have not found.

It's very frustrating to try to talk to men and women who feel this way. They are running away from love and don't even realize it. There is one thing all people with commitment conflicts have in common. They all expect love to hit them with complete certitude. They all believe that commitment begins with the "right partner," the person who will make them feel embraced, loved, and part of a special universe. Some people search the globe, looking for the right partner; others stay home and dream about the right partner finding them. Neither of these methods works.

People with commitment issues often carry the same attitude into other areas of their lives. They are always searching for the perfect job, the perfect apartment, or even the perfect pair of shoes. They are resistent to *all* forms of commitment, and they avoid decisions from which they feel there is no turning back.

I'm not saying this so that you can start beating yourself up for your failures. I am saying this so you will *stop* beating yourself up—and stop beating others up as well. The sooner you place your conflicts out on the table, in full sight, the sooner you can begin to dismantle them. Change is possible.

GOING FROM BLAME TO RESPONSIBILITY

The road to love and commitment begins when you stop running away from your own conflicts. Not when you meet the right person. Not when you become monogamous. Not when you get engaged. Not when you get married. Not when you have your first child; and not when you celebrate your silver anniversary. It begins when you stop blaming the partners who have failed you and fess up and assume responsibility for the way *you* have handled *your* relationships.

Start by Looking at How You Make Your Connections

There are three big questions to ask yourself:

- How Do *I* Set *Myself* Up for Disappointment?
- How Do *I* Set Other People Up for Disappointment?
- How Could *I* Do Something Different in the Future?

These questions can be applied to just about any situation. Recently I did a radio call-in show, and one of the woman listeners called in to talk about her romantic history. Here's part of what she said:

"The last three men I've been involved with have all been afraid. But the last one was the worst. I thought for sure we were going to be life partners but then he did practically an overnight, 180-degree turn in what seems to be an unpredictable fashion and ended things. I want to know what it is about me that enables this to happen? Why do guys like this find me?"

I'm asked variations on this question fairly often. And I think that this woman and others like her are asking the wrong question. If people with serious commitment issues continue to cross your path, remember: There's a lot of this going around. If you walk out the door, there is an amazingly good chance that you will find potential partners who can't sustain real relationships. The issue is not why they are finding you, but why *you are getting involved*. Instead of focusing on all the problematic people in the world, it's time to start thinking about how your *own* patterns could be changed.

The First BIG Question to Ask Yourself Is: *How Do I Set Myself Up for Disappointment?*

It's no fun to be walking around feeling like a confused victim. And it's almost impossible to get to commitment if you keep making the same errors in judgment. Do you want to get a handle on how you set yourself up for romantic disappointment? Typically it happens in one or all of the following ways.

1. Not paying enough attention to your own romantic history and needs.

You are the best person to understand your own behavior. Only you know exactly how vulnerable you might be to a certain kind of attention courtship and seduction. Do you have a tendency to not be properly self-protective? Did you ever let a relationship proceed too quickly or get intimate too fast? When you meet a potential partner, do you stop for a moment and listen to the wise little warning voice in your head, or do you just barge forward and hope for the best? Do you have a series of lame rationales that have failed you in the past, such as "How do I know if I can trust somebody until I trust him (her)?"

Pay careful attention to the lessons of your own life. If, for example, you have ever been involved in a relationship that came with built-in distance because your partner was married, chronically unfaithful, or geographically or emotionally unavailable, face the fact that you may choose relationships with built-in distance.

We all need to be more self-protective and keep our emotional and physical boundaries in place until we *know*—not hope—that things will work out.

2. Not discovering or paying attention to your potential partner's relationship history.

If someone has had commitment conflicts in the past, he or she will almost inevitably have them in the future. Find out your partner's relationship history before you give away your heart. You don't have to overwhelm a first date with a barrage of questions. Just let your connections develop naturally, and you'll find out. People talk; their friends and relatives talk. You don't have to pry; you don't have to be accusatory or judgmental. All you have to do is listen and ask a few *gentle* questions, and you'll find out what you need to know. And if you hear or see something that sounds like there could be trouble, pay attention, and be self-protective.

Donna, a woman I once interviewed, said that her boyfriend was so afraid of commitment that he broke their engagement by e-mail. She says that nothing about his behavior in the beginning of the relationship gave her any warning. "There must have been something," I said. "Well," she answered, "on our first date in a very expensive restaurant, this good looking woman was seated at another table. When Gerald saw her, he said 'uh-oh.' Then this woman walked up to our table, sat down, and said, 'you've been ignoring me for five months. I thought we had a relationship. Are you ever going to give me an explanation for what happened?'"

"So," I asked Donna, "Didn't this make you at all worried that he might someday make you as angry as he had made this other woman?"

As Donna continued talking, she remembered numerous other stories that Gerald had told her about how he had run away from relationships with other women in his past. She simply failed to pay attention.

3. Believing (a) you are special and (b) your relationship will be so special that common sense doesn't apply.

Some of us have been waiting our entire lives for that special someone. Inappropriately romantic, we fall in love with love. We want to believe that our connection is so special that it is touched with magic. When we look at other people who are being unrealistic, we can see how they are messing up. In our own lives, however, we think all the rules can be broken.

Donna, for example, could see that Gerald might have been unkind to the woman who barged into their dinner, but she was so wrapped up in the romantic dynamic she and Gerald shared that she couldn't see that he might also be unkind to her. Yes, of course we can't all walk through the world with a completely cynical and negative point of view. And people do change. Even Gerald may change some day. But typically they change only because there has been a major life event that alters their outlook, or they change because they are fully committed to doing so.

4. Not paying attention early on to a partner's double messages.

I like to say that people with commitment issues come with disclaimers. Typically they are always doing or saying something that is a clear warning. Often they say it up front loudly, as in, "My ex-wife/girlfriend/family, etc., all say I can't make a commitment," or "Watch out for me," or "I can't really be trusted," or "I never seem to be able to stay interested," or even "I'm in a bad marriage."

It's easy not to pay sufficient attention to these kinds of messages, particularly because your potential partner is probably showering you with affection and attention. We all tend to pay attention to the positive behavior and hope or assume that the reservations are temporary or that they will go away. This is a big mistake.

Double messages are part and parcel of commitmentphobic relationships. The partner with active conflicts is almost always saying yes and no at the same time. He or she may be showering you with intimate, loving words at the same time that he or she is also creating excessive boundaries that keep you from getting too close. The problem with these mixed messages is that more often than not, they are both equally true.

People with commitment conflicts are often genuinely of two minds. One mind wants in—often quite desperately. The other wants out—often just as desperately. If you are involved with such a person, you have to hear *both* messages—the distancing negative as well as the passionate positive. To be appropriately self-protective, it would be a good idea to pay as much attention to the negative behavior as you do the positive.

5. Ignoring reality and not paying enough attention to what is happening in the present.

Reality testing is very important. A question to ask yourself is whether your relationships have been satisfying moment by moment. Have they made you happy day by day? Have they been nurturing and supportive? Or do you create myths about what is taking place?

It's always a mistake to let your dreams, your fantasies, or your partner's promises of a rosy future become more important than everyday reality. It also goes without saying that living in the past is not the way to find the love you want.

It can take a lot of courage to face the full picture of your relationships. But it's worth it.

6. Allowing yourself to be swept up in someone else's romantic agenda even when you feel he or she is being unrealistic.

"She said she thought she was falling in love on our first date."

"He had been married three times, but he made me feel like he had never been in love before."

"The day after we met, she sent me a half dozen cute faxes telling me how wonderful she thought I was."

"I didn't even like him that much; he just wore me down with sheer persistence."

I've said it before, and I'm sure I'll say it again: Often the only people who are brave enough to be so totally shameless about their romantic agendas are those who have had a lot of practice. I'm not against romance. I think it's wonderful. I am, however, very suspicious of completely unrealistic pursuits.

If you live your life believing that someday you will have a "great" love, you can be a pushover for the first person who employs "great love language" or behavior. You can believe that your dreams are being fulfilled, even if there is little follow through and essential real elements are missing.

People are frequently advised to "follow their hearts," instead of their heads. I think this is one of the most misguided messages in the world. I don't want to sound cynical here. I believe there's a lot of room for heart in a relationship. I just need to make it clear here that people who say they are following their hearts are usually following their fantasies and their hormones. The heart connection takes time to develop, and it's really quite subtle. Our fantasies and our hormones, on the other hand, typically have all the subtlety of King Kong.

7. Failing to maintain appropriate boundaries.

Some of us are so needy for love that we give away too much, too soon. We get worried that unless we are 100 percent accepting, giving, and loving, we might be rejected. We open our hearts, our doors, our refrigerators, and sometimes even our checkbooks. We place few limits, and little or nothing is held back.

How do we do this? Here's a partial list: We let strangers into our lives too quickly; we fail to be adequately self-protective; we give more than is being asked—or being given; we risk too much in the name of love. We change our religions and our occupations; we move our residence; we redecorate and buy new furniture to suit someone else's needs; we inappropriately share our resources; we prioritize someone else's needs above our own; sometimes we even abandon our friends, give away our pets, and change the way we relate to our children.

One minute we feel like men and women with lives of our own; the next we feel as though we are doing nothing but accommodating. What makes this behavior even more self-defeating is that frequently the recipient knows that he or she hasn't earned it and may even question your behavior or doubt your sincerity.

Remember, if you give 10,000 percent before you know if a relationship warrants so much giving, you have no place to go but backward.

The Second BIG Question to Ask Yourself Is: *How Do I Set Others Up for Disappointment?*

Some people hurt themselves by hurting others. It's no fun walking around feeling both guilty and confused. Do you want to get a handle on how you might set others up for romantic disappointment? Typically it happens in one or all of the following ways.

1. Not paying enough attention to your own romantic history and needs.

Only you know how many times you have worn down a potential partner's boundaries and defenses with extreme romantic gestures and language—only to decide later that you weren't that interested in pursuing anything further. Have you ever initially pursued someone even though there were a thousand little voices telling you that this person wasn't right for you—voices that you didn't start listening to until after you made the conquest?

If you have commitment conflicts, you are probably aware of them. If you are capable of dating more than one person at a time while making each of them feel that he or she is the only one, you know it better than anybody. You can't go through life assuming that your partners will take care of themselves. It almost inevitably backfires.

2. Not paying enough attention to your potential partner's relationship history and emotional makeup.

Take a good look at the person you are trying to impress. Will he or she be seriously disappointed—more disappointed than you—if the relationship you are trying to establish goes awry? Is he or she visibly vulnerable? Does he or she have some overriding element that is creating greater vulnerability, such as a history of emotional distress, a recent disastrous romance, small dependent children, or current life problems?

I once interviewed a man who told me that he felt particularly guilty about a woman he had recently stopped seeing. Early on in their relationship she had turned to him and said, "Promise me one thing. That no matter what happens, you won't lie to me." And he, responding to the intense emotionality of the moment, made that promise. "And then?" I asked. "And then I lied to her. Oh shit," he said, "I was probably already lying to her."

3. Believing you have to sell yourself and your specialness.

You may have a tendency to treat potential partners as though they are "buyers" to whom you are "pitching" your wares. What you fail to consider is that you are not a new (or used) car. When you have made the sale, you may not be prepared to hand over the keys. Yet the intensity of your charm and the implicit promise that is part and parcel of your sales pitch is designed to make someone believe that you are already prepared to do just that once he or she says "yes."

Some salespeople may focus more on the pitch and on what they are selling than on their customers. In fact, they sometimes even depersonalize their customers. Unfortunately, in the romantic arena, this attitude comes with some serious problems: The partner to whom you have been "selling" your product has received three messages from your pitch...

1. Wow, he/she is so special.
2. Wow, he/she likes me so much; I must be special too.
3. Wow, together we are going to have one heck of a special relationship.

Don't be surprised if the person to whom you have been "selling" your specialness is upset if you don't follow through. To this person, it can feel as though a major emotional contract has been broken. In truth, your own insecurity may be the reason why you continue to sell your own "specialness" or value to a prospective partner. Typically your partners are aware of your insecurity. Often this just strengthens the appeal—it makes you appear even more sensitive and attractive.

4. Not understanding that you are giving your partner two separate and distinct messages.

Recently a male caller on a radio show told me that he couldn't understand why women expected more of him than he was prepared to give. He said, "Women keep falling for me, and I don't know why since I always warn them not to get serious."

I remember saying to him, "I accept the fact that you give them this warning, and I accept on face value that a lot of people can't hear warnings, and instead see them as challenges. But I have to ask you: Is there anything else that you might do that might confuse them. Are you incredibly seductive?"

He said that he had to admit that he knocked himself out to please a woman. He bought women he barely knew presents, took them to great places, and was a very passionate, considerate lover. He enjoyed turning women on. And he did.

The moral of this story: If you pull out all the stops in the romance department, don't be surprised if your partner feels cared for in a special way. This is not the behavior of someone who just wants to have a few laughs. It's confusing as well as seductive.

Actually I've known many people—both male and female— who articulated a predicament similar to this radio-show caller. I always remember Doug, a thirty-five-year-old accountant who moved in with his girlfriend and spent all his weekends playing with her two kids, who he really loved. Because of his behavior, his girlfriend thought the relationship had a future. Doug thought he made himself clear because of the many times he said, "I'm not sure about what I want."

Some men and women, of course, are very careful not to *do* anything that might indicate that a relationship has a future. Frequently, however, they are not so cautious about their *words*. I interviewed a woman once who told me that her boyfriend phoned her an average of three times a day to say that he loved her, but he wouldn't include her in any social events because that implied a commitment he wasn't ready to make.

If your own confusion about what you want causes you to give double messages, bear in mind that your partners are human; they are going to hear the messages they want to hear and disregard the rest. In the meantime, the relationship gets stuck in the extreme ends of either message; it becomes like a rollercoaster with no true center.

5. Ignoring reality and fooling yourself into believing that your actions don't have consequences.

If you are living with someone, it's real; you have a relationship.

If you are seeing someone a couple of times a week for a period of six months or more, it's real; you have a relationship.

If you share your secrets and your thoughts with someone on a regular basis, it's real; you have a relationship.

If you have encouraged intimacy and trust, it's real; you have a relationship.

Have you ever convinced yourself that you don't have a relationship, when it's simply not true? Have you ever told yourself that your partner understands that it's not serious, when it's simply not true?

Face facts: For you to believe that you can seamlessly move in and out of another person's life is unrealistic. That's your fantasy. The reality is that you're going to suffer, and your partner is probably going to suffer more.

6. Saying and doing things that build expectations without following through on your promises.

I certainly understand how easy it is to get carried away and caught up in a romantic pursuit. I understand how easy it is to let things go too far. And I understand how sincere it can feel while you are doing it. But I also know the feeling of waking up the next morning when the adrenaline has worn off and thinking, "My God, what have I done?"

If your romantic behavior and the possible consequences of this behavior has ever scared you out of your own skin, then you need to step back and evaluate your style. Think about all you've done to encourage intimacy and trust. Think about all the times you couldn't take no for an answer...until someone said yes. In all honesty, no one is asking you to push this hard. But once you have, the person who you have been pursuing may well believe what you've said and done. You need to take things more slowly.

7. Having boundaries that come and go in response to circumstances.

When you are trying to win someone over, you may be capable of spinning such a romantic cocoon that it appears as though there is nothing between you and your partner, and everything between the two of you and the world. Then, whoa, your needs change, and you can erect such enormous boundaries that your partner feels completely left out. Are you capable of appearing passionate, warm, and connected one minute, and withdrawn, withholding, and downright cold the next?

I recently met someone who told me that his "girlfriend" spent at least four sexually charged nights a week at his apartment. Nonetheless, she didn't want him visiting in her space, and she didn't want to do anything in public—like go to a movie—for fear he might get the wrong idea. In other words sometimes this woman wants to be so close that nothing can come between them; other times she creates enormous distance by erecting huge, unscalable boundaries.

Many men and women with commitment conflicts frequently want to have it both ways. Sometimes they want an intimate relationship; sometimes they want that relationship to disappear. They handle these two opposing desires by pulling down and putting up boundaries.

The Third BIG Question to Ask Yourself Is: *How Can I Do Something Different in the Future?*

There is, of course, an obvious answer: Become aware and conscious of what you have done in the past, and don't repeat your patterns. If you change for the better, so will your relationships.

When it comes to creating more fulfilling future relationships, I want you to know that I understand that some people really don't want things to be different. "I want this to change," they tell me. "I'm ready for something healthier." "I'm ready for love," they say. The words leave their mouths, but they don't land in fertile soil; they don't take root and produce new behavior. The language is there, but there is no real commitment to change. Given that commitment is the organizing problem here, I guess this should come as no surprise.

If it is your most sincere wish to find and hold on to meaningful love in your life, this is a struggle that has to be taken seriously. *You* have to really want it. *You* have to really change. Ten years ago I wanted my life to be different, but I still believed that time and circumstances would make the changes for me. I believed time and circumstances would bring me new partners and new outcomes. I thought that time and circumstances would bring me the future I desired, and all I needed to do was wait. So I waited. And I waited. And I watched as nothing really changed.

If you change for the better, so will your relationships

The first thing I think you can do is get a sense of how real relationships work. Relationships are not a result of magic and wishful thinking. They *always* take time and excellent intentions on the part of both partners. There are *always* dozens of issues, both large and small, to be ironed out *before* two people can know whether they should be together. There are *always* dozens of issues to be ironed out *after* two people decide to be together. Committed relationships don't happen magically. You start working on your relationships by making a commitment to work on yourself.

The Courage to Say Good-bye to Your Ghosts

Often before we can form committed relationships, we have to examine the personal material that has created problems in the past. I have a woman friend named Angela who talks a fair amount about what she calls her "relationship history." A year ago, Angela rejected the man she lived with and was engaged to marry so she could be with the person she thinks of as the "great love" of her life. Soon thereafter her great love "dumped" her, as she puts it, for somebody else. She says it is going to take her more than a year to sort out what really happened. Why, she wonders, did she walk out on her fiancé? Why did she fall in love with somebody else? Was it just momentary madness created by the idea of a marriage? Why did her new love, in turn, reject her a week after she ended her engagement? Angela says that these days she often feels depressed and lonely. In fact, she feels haunted by her memories. But she isn't sure exactly who it is she misses. Does she miss her fiancé and the stable life they shared? Does she miss the "great love" who turned out to be the great abandoner? Or does she, as her therapist has suggested, really miss the mother who left her with a series of babysitters from the time she was just an infant?

By the time we are old enough and wise enough to be capable of entering into a mature, loving relationship, most of us are already carrying around a fair amount of history. This history surrounds us with what I call "ghosts." We all have our share of them.

If you are reading this book, undoubtedly you want to understand more about your own story. You want to know why you've made less than ideal romantic choices; you want to know why you keep coming up empty-handed. Gaining greater insight into who your ghosts are and why they exist will help you get a better picture of who you are and why you behave the way you do. When it comes to relationships, they say hindsight is always twenty-twenty. I like to say that insight supplants the need for hindsight.

CONNECTING IN THE PRESENT = CONNECTING TO THE PAST

For some people, connecting to another human being appears to be a fairly simple process of going out for dinner and a movie. Then there's some pleasant conversation, a few laughs, a walk along a beach, some hand-holding, a kiss that leads to another kiss, and then, next thing you know, RELATIONSHIP. Why should it be any more complicated than that. Why? Because for better or worse, we are far more complicated than that.

Psychologists tell us that the struggle to connect in the present is totally dependent upon and dictated by struggles with connection in the past. When we are weighed down by burdens from the past, we are rarely totally "free" to connect with our partners; we connect only as much as our past struggles allow.

In a nutshell, in order to make and sustain a new loving connection, your mind and your heart must, and will, revisit all past connections. When you start a new relationship, you automatically begin an internal stroll down memory lane. Like it or not, as new emotions are stirred, you emotionally revisit every relationship, both loving and hurtful, that you have ever had. This means every single friendship and every single foeship; every triumph and every tear; every failure and every fantasy.

And if this already sounds like a lot of emotional pot-stirring, understand that this revisiting process is not limited to relationships that started with your first bout of puppy love. You will revisit your connections with your parents, siblings, and, other childhood caregivers from the moment you were born (if we accept studies on in-utero bondings between twins, perhaps even *before* your were born). Think about how you related with your mother, father, sisters and brothers, aunts, uncles, grandmothers and grandfathers, housekeepers, babysitters, neighbors, and friends—present and absent, dead and alive. If someone touched your life, you may find this presence haunting your current relationships, and until you make some peace with your past, it will happen again and again and again and again.

The emotional 'supercomputer' that lives inside of you will retrieve this information from your memory banks so quickly and efficiently that the results may be positively overwhelming. The emotional inventory that takes place in every new situation is not something we do by choice. It is automatic, and it is unavoidable. To make matters even more complex, very little of it may be conscious. This process of revisiting your past can be out of your control unless you take clear and concrete steps. Becoming more familiar with the various emotional ghosts you carry from the past can help you become more aware and free to find more loving relationships in the present and future.

It Takes Courage to Face Your Ghosts

Just about everything we know about love and commitment, we learned from our ghosts. Some people are very fortunate. They have wonderful childhoods surrounded by loving caregivers and peers. When they reach adulthood, they date an appropriate number of years before falling in love and getting married. When these people think about the past, they don't feel haunted. Instead they feel very supported by consistent memories of loving connections. Many more of us, however, have backgrounds that include at least a few ghosts that we would rather leave behind. These ghosts represent the losses, experiences, and events that freeze us in our tracks and thus keep us from being able to move forward in loving relationships.

Ignoring these ghosts doesn't make them disappear. Although we may not feel them haunting us twenty-four hours a day, they pop up when we least want them—short circuiting our ability to move forward in good relationships. They pop up when the phone rings or doesn't ring; they pop up when we ask for a date or reach for a kiss; they pop up when we walk hand-in-hand in the park; and they even pop up when we walk to the altar. Our ghosts show up every time we try to make a loving connection. It would appear that the only way we can make our ghosts vanish is by facing them realistically and seeing them for what they are. Let's take a look at some of the emotional ghosts we find making "booooo" sounds in our lives.

The Ghosts of Yesterday's Loves

We are now living in a time when it is considered par for the course to have a few or even many relationships before we marry. Think about all the details you've had to remember about each of your partners—his/her birthday, his/her sweater size, not to mention what he/she puts in a cup of coffee. Small wonder that by the time we finally settle down with one life partner, we still find ghosts of all these other people with their different preferences, love-making styles, and personal peculiarities hanging around.

Get some perspective on your ghosts by taking a trip down memory lane with an emphasis on your own romantic history. Think about the connections you've made and the losses you've experienced. Whether they were many or few, these memories are filled with emotion. Think about the first crush, the fifth crush, the umpteenth crush, the summer flings, the winter flings, the fall and spring flings. How about your first date, first kiss, and all the dates and kisses that followed? There may have been fiancées and spouses, and at least one "love of my life." Whether these relationships ended badly or not so badly (whatever that means), haven't we all experienced endings and losses?

People like to believe that the past is the past, but nothing fully recedes into the past until you have processed it and put it to rest. If, for example, you have a complex history filled with losses

nothing fully recedes into the past until you have processed it and put it to rest

that have not been fully processed or grieved, these losses can fill you with discomfort, anxiety, even a sense of dread every time you try to make a new connection.

When we lose a loved one through the break up of a relationship, we don't always grieve in appropriate ways. Sometimes we nostalgically hang on to the memory of these lost connections far too long; other times we blot out the memory of people we loved as though they never existed. There is a reason why so many recovery programs stress the importance of forgiveness and making amends. The creators of these programs know too well how hard it is to move forward when you have not made peace with your past.

I know that I found it extremely healing to construct a graph of all my past relationships and write down the feelings I had at the end of each relationship with special attention paid to becoming aware of how those feelings helped determine what I then did. I started back in seventh grade. This, my first little romance, was a less than positive experience. This memory began in the schoolyard at recess when a female classmate approached me to say that another girl in my class—I don't remember her name, but let's call her Nancy—*really* liked me. I was immediately flattered. Then after lunch, this same messenger said that Nancy wanted to know if I liked her back. "Sure," I said, not knowing what that meant.

That afternoon, sitting in class, I received a note. Once again, it was the same go-between. The note said. "Nancy wants to know if you want to go steady. If you do, send her your ID bracelet." This seemed vaguely thrilling and very grown up. I remember wrapping my ID bracelet in paper, putting it in an envelope, and sending it across the class to Nancy's desk. She looked at me and smiled. I smiled back. We were going steady! Wow!

The next day, my ID bracelet came back to me in exactly the same way—wrapped in paper in an envelope. Nancy had rejected me. It had ended as quickly as it had begun. I hadn't even noticed her before she picked me out, but now I couldn't help but be aware of her presence. I felt humiliated and hurt. I clearly remember determining that I would be more careful in the future.

When I pulled up my romantic ghosts and made a list starting with this failed connection, I could clearly see how my feelings at the end of each relationship helped change my behavior and attitude, and thus helped determine what happened next. Some of this was very subtle. In many instances, it was extraordinarily obvious. Men and women who have followed my suggestion have had a similar experience.

• Julian says that a college romance left him feeling so mortified that he immediately jumped into a "boring" marriage with the first woman who flattered his ego.

- When Jamie's engagement ended, she felt like a vulnerable and undesirable failure. Believing that another man might help her erase these feelings, she started dating with a vengeance. At an office party when she found herself responding to the advances of a man she didn't even like, she realized that something was very wrong with her behavior.

This is all very obvious and almost embarrassingly simplistic pop psychology. Yet, when it happens to us, even though what is happening is blatantly apparent, we don't fully think through the experience. We don't work our feelings out. To hide from our painful feelings, typically we immediately focus on finding another partner—or even ways of reclaiming the old partner. We don't learn our lessons. And thus history tends to repeat itself time and again.

The Ghost of Unforgettable Love

Some ex-loves take on such mythic proportions that they deserve a ghost category all their own. Many people have told me how difficult it is for them to stop wallowing in romantic memories and move on. I personally know at least two women and one man who have mourned specific failed relationships for years and years. One of these women recently told me that she has reached the point where she is genuinely embarrassed to tell anyone that she can't get over her ex-husband whom she hasn't even seen in eight years. How does this happen? Why does this happen?

I've noticed that people who continue to hang on to the memory of one particular partner tend to be confused about the nature of love itself. They get their belief in love entangled with their belief in a specific partner, and they can't separate the two.

One woman actually said to me, "I love Kyle so much that this relationship has to work out; otherwise I will stop believing in love." For a short time, "Kyle" made her feel completely loved in a way that she only dreamed about. Even though Kyle's love proved to be superficial despite all his declarations, she just wants to go back to the way she felt when the relationship was at its best. She hangs on to this memory, like a very small child clings to his parents for protection.

Some people feel only longing for their ex-partners. Others experience a fearful combination of love and hate, depression and anger, desire and disgust. If you are trying to get over a relationship, I know that it's an indescribably painful experience. Numerous books have been written about the grieving process, and they can be very helpful—if you are even able to begin to process the loss. Even more helpful, and often absolutely necessary, is to get yourself to a counselor, therapist, or support group. You may find it helpful to consult with an MD, either a psychiatrist or your own general practitioner to see if a course of antidepressant medication is warranted.

Many people who enter therapy do so at just such moments. I know firsthand because that's what happened to me. I discovered, as have many others, that you can use this difficult time as a great opportunity to access the deeper memories that are fueling your pain and keeping you from moving on.

The Greater Ghosts of Childhood

"Oh, my God," my friend Sheila shrieked in my ear. *"I've married my mother. Okay, he's taller, and he fights with me instead of my father. But otherwise, he's exactly the same."*

Our first romantic relationships were with our early caregivers. These were the first people with whom we opened our hearts, the first people to whom we gave our trust. Look at the eyes of an infant as it stares into the eyes of its mother. If that is not love, what is? Look at the two-year-old girl clinging unashamedly to her dad. If that is not love, what is? Look at the young brother and sister holding hands, and the toddler playing with a grandparent. Listen to the way a six-year-old girl talks about her teacher. The vulnerability of the heart in these early connections is unique, and never the same once our defenses build. Anything that affects your ability to get close to another human being shapes your future. And these greater ghosts, the ghosts of your deepest past, affect your ability the most. Too many negative experiences when we are still children, and we are left with little courage to love.

Too many negative experiences and we are left with little courage to love

No matter how idyllic your childhood, your earliest connections will almost inevitably present you with at least a few stubborn and intractable ghosts. Your parents may have been very loving and communicative with each other, but how about their capacity to connect with you? Your parents may have been very loving to you, but what about the example they were setting in their interactions with each other? What about sibling issues? Did you and your brothers and sisters get along?

Many of us grew up with parents who were emotionally or physically absent, overly anxious, faultfinding, controlling, angry, resentful, overly burdened, financially stressed. All of these situations create their very own special hauntings. Years later we find ourselves keeping house with someone who pushes the same buttons our parents pushed; years later we find qualities in ourselves that more than anything resemble parental qualities that we didn't like; years later we find ourselves behaving with our mates as we once behaved with our siblings.

Ghosts Who Belong to a Special Time and Place

Louise says that she was fifty years old before she realized that many of her relationship choices could be traced to the effects of World War II. Louise spent the first five years of her life in a small midwestern town where most of the men were at war. This experience provided her with powerful memories of women who were alternately anticipating a loved one's return and worrying whether he would return. Until she was in her mid-thirties, Louise regularly formed relationships with men who were either married or lived great distances away. Like the women in her family during the war, Louise's relationships were marked by passionate reunions and painful separations.

If you grew up in the suburbs where many of the parents, particularly the men, left for work every morning and took a late commuter train home every night, you're going to have a different view of the way people connect than if you grew up on a farm or with parents who worked together in a small mom-and-pop–type operation.

We have all been affected by the events and mood of the times in which we grew up. Segregation, the civil rights movement, the Vietnam War, the peace movement, folk music, rock and roll, drugs, the women's liberation movement, the sexual revolution, and even new age spirituality have all left behind ghosts, both good and bad, that influence the way we form partnerships. So have movies, television shows, books, and anything else that helped shape the morals and ideas of their times.

The Ghosts of Christmas Past

In Dickens' *A Christmas Carol,* Ebeneezer Scrooge is haunted by the Ghost of Christmas Past. Like him, we all have ghosts that show up specifically for the holidays or other special occasions. These hauntings cross ethnic and religious lines. They happen at Kwanzaa, Rosh Hashanah, Ramadan as well as birthdays, anniversaries, Valentine's Day, New Year's Day, Mother's Day, Father's Day, and even the 4th of July. You get the picture.

I have been interviewing people about their relationships for more than ten years, and there is one consistent theme in these interviews: The degree to which people "charge" their holiday celebrations. Many magazine and newspaper articles have already been written describing the unrealistic expectations and subsequent disappointments we experience during holidays. What we rarely stop to consider is how we often use holidays to measure the success or failure of our relationships and how we judge partners by how they celebrate special occasions. "I'll give this relationship until Christmas or the New Year," is an expression I've heard regularly.

Sometimes we even end relationships because of something that did or didn't happen on one special time or another. Did we feel everything we thought we should feel for Valentine's Day? Did he/she celebrate our birthday the way we anticipated? Men and women with commitment issues, for example, quite often end their relationships just before family holidays such as Thanksgiving or Christmas. Typically they say that they don't want their intentions to be misconstrued; they don't want anyone to get the idea that the relationship is permanent.

The Large Personal Trauma Ghosts

Dorothy's mother became bed-ridden before Dorothy entered first grade.

Jonathan's father was an abusive alcoholic.

Rebekka's father abandoned the family when Rebekka was an infant.

Carlos had a serious childhood illness that required lonely months in a hospital as well as several terrifying surgeries.

Eileen's sister died when Eileen was six.

Some of us have histories that contain at least one major trauma or loss that regularly comes back to haunt us. The younger we were, the more likely we are to bury the emotional distress we saw and felt. Young children don't have the skills or understanding to handle losses; they don't have sophisticated ways of grieving. Childhood losses are rarely processed; instead they are collected and stored. The "ghosts" of parents who were abusive, inappropriately sexual, overly critical, demanding, guilt provoking, smothering, unavailable, or absent—to name just a few—are with us for all of our lives.

Some people don't like looking into their childhood to explain why their personal relationships so often go askew. "The past is the past," they say. "What's done is done." "Everyone has *some* problem." "I want to move forward, not look back." The problem is that what is done is not done at all, and it can be your personal undoing. As adults we sometimes continue to hide from the pain we felt as children by avoiding relationships that make us feel vulnerable. We look for "safe" solutions with partners who don't demand connection or unavailable partners who never get too close for too long. If we manage accidently to stumble into something loving, we may experience a generalized anxiety we can't really explain; we may become uncomfortable when things feel too good for too long.

Many of us can entertain the troops with our bizarre war stories about our dysfunctional, trauma-inducing, or overly burdened families as well as our horror stories about past relationships. But there is a big difference between having a rote knowledge of these stories and being emotionally connected to their content and significance.

When a child is bitten by a dog, we understand that child's subsequent fear. Same thing if someone is stung by a bee. I have a friend who once walked around the corner in her office and was hit in the chin by a golf club—a co-worker was practicing his swing. Years later she was walking down a busy metropolitan street. As she rounded a corner, her eye spotted a spring display in a department store window, featuring two male dummies swinging golf clubs. She says she immediately jumped back as though she had been hit once again.

The same thing happens with love. If we have tried to open our hearts to love only to be hit in the face with a symbolic golf club, we carry that memory with us, forgetting that it's even there. We frequently package these memories so carefully that we lose the ability to access and recognize the pain. We become disconnected from our experience. But that doesn't mean that we stop carrying those memories and the defense systems that go along with them. Some of these memories can only be accessed and worked through in therapy. Others are bubbling along the surface. We know they are there; we simply don't acknowledge their power.

The human spirit is incredibly resilient, capable of handling losses and recovering. But as children, we don't always have the luxury of being able to fully process loss. We were just too young. So we develop primitive strategies for grieving, or complete denial strategies that contain our anguish. We typically learn these strategies from family styles—styles that encourage you to "get over it," "snap out of it," or "look at the positive" (without acknowledging the negative). The more we contain our pain, the more we build a wall of defense against further losses.

Fantasy Ghosts

Do you remember your earliest romantic and/or sexual fantasies? As you matured, did they alter dramatically in tone and content? Probably not.

Benjamin says that his father, who had an awful temper, was emotionally abusive to the whole family, particularly his mother. In his childhood fantasies, Benjamin was a superhero who was able to come to his mother's aid and teach his father a lesson. To this day, Benjamin is attracted to women in trouble.

Debra says that she met her first love in a playpen when she was a baby. He was the baby boy next door. When she was five, he and his family moved away. It was utter heartbreak. To complicate matters, the day before the family moved, her little boyfriend fell and broke his arm—his right arm. Every night before she fell asleep, she would think about this little boy. She would fantasize about how they would grow up and get married, and how she would help him get around with his broken arm. In these fantasies he would be very dependent on, and grateful for, her loving care. These were her first caretaker fantasies. As an adult, she has continued her caretaker and reunion fantasies. Many of her adult relationships, not surprisingly, have been with unavailable men, and in most of these unions, she has played the role of caretaker or responsible adult.

As children if we are not getting the quality of love we want, we frequently retreat into fantasies to fill the void and help heal our emotional wounds; these fantasies or daydreams give us a sense of power that as children we don't have. As we mature, our daydreams stay with us, evolving as we evolve. In these days, fantasy figures are frequently based on real people, but there is a crucial difference. In our fantasies, *we are always in control of what happens.* These fantasy ghost figures are so satisfying. However, they can stop us from moving forward as adults because they make it difficult for us to work with flesh and blood potential.

Unlike real partners, who may be too tall, short, overweight, underweight, talkative, uncommunicative, etc., fantasy partners always want to give us what we want; they always want to do what we want; **THEY ALWAYS WANT FROM US EXACTLY WHAT WE WANT TO GIVE.** These fantasy partners become ghostlike presences in our lives. They travel with us to give us comfort and satisfaction wherever we go.

With a fantasy partner, you can have a perfect match. In fact, a critical attitude frequently comes from holding real partners up to ideals they can't possibly meet. The cornerstone of the faultfinding mechanism is the belief that perfection exists. This belief can only come out of fantasy.

How Ghosts From the Past May Be Embedded in Your Programming

Your ghosts are probably influencing how you choose your partners, how you behave with your partners, and even how you and your partners spend the holidays. So are you starting to feel like a haunted house on Halloween? Are you seeing ghosts everywhere you turn? Is there anything you can do about this?

The "work" around ghost material is work that can most easily be done in the office of a competent therapist. For me, taking the therapeutic road was an important step in my emotional growth. But through the experience of my own therapy and witnessing the experience of so many others, it has also become clear that even the most exhaustive "ghost-busting" does not necessarily guarantee a new and different beginning. We can continue to make the same mistakes and the same foolish choices. Even if we are certain we are no longer afraid of love, we can continue going round and round in the same kind of self-destructive relationship loops.

Why does this happen? It happens because the ghosts from our past have programmed us how to behave in the future. And these "programs" act like complex software—ghost software, if you will—that continues to "run" in our systems even if the ghosts are long gone. Some of us are programmed to be difficult and moody; some of us are programmed to keep everything "on the surface"; some of us are programmed to be highly flirtatious; some of us are programmed to be caustic and critical; some of us are programmed to be unfaithful; some of us are programmed to be more tolerant of abuse; some of us are programmed to be contemptuous of the opposite sex; some of us are programmed to be contemptuous of our own sex.

ghosts from our past have programmed us how to behave in the future

All of these programs act like giant obstructions that keep us from getting any further on the road to love. They disconnect us from our true feelings; disconnect us from our true selves; and disconnect us from the people we choose as partners. The crucial thing for you to understand about your programming is that these are only ghost programs. This is not who you are; it is what you have learned. What has been learned can also be unlearned; you *can* find better programs. Start by becoming very conscious of who you are and how you behave in relationships. Without activating ghost voices that encourage you to blame or beat up on yourself, you might start by regularly asking yourself, "Why do I want that?" "Why did I say that?" "Why did I do that?" If there is one place where you have the power to make changes right now, it is in the area of your own programming. By understanding how your programs work to help you or hinder you, you can become your own software specialist.

Ghosts program your choices as well as your behavior. Let's look at some of the most common programs and how they keep us from having the love we want.

Programmed to Be Judgmental and Picky

Were you born into a family that notices *everything*? If that's the case, when it comes to choosing life partners, you may go through life hearing the often disparaging ghost voices of one or both parents. "What does she do for a living? Is that a normal job?" "He/she certainly knows how to eat." "I anticipate a weight problem later on." "She/he is too short/tall/fat /thin/conservative/liberal/career oriented/lacking in ambition." Sometimes these voices have an approving tone. "He/she is so successful/rich/smart." "He/she has such a great apartment/house/car/hairstyle." "He/she has such great taste/friends/vacations." But what is it that these voices are approving of and are these things that we want to value?

Of course, ghost voices sometimes remind us to notice really important positive characteristics. If your family regularly stressed loving/caring/thoughtful, you may have been very self-protectively programmed to look for these qualities in a mate. Quite often, however, our programming is merely superficial.

Many of the members of my immediate family, for example, are quite tall, and growing up I remember a fair amount of discussion about how good it was to be tall, and how much less desirable it was to be short. Many of the women I dated were also tall. From a logical point of view, this might make sense given my height. However, when I started to get very serious about my wife, who is very petite, I found these messages messing up my head. I was deeply in love, and yet I was considering her height. It was ludicrous.

Programmed to Do the Opposite of What Your Parents Did

They lived in the suburbs, so I'll live in the city.

They want me to date someone who is Catholic/Protestant/Jewish/Muslim/Buddhist so I'll make sure I never even talk to anyone who fits this description.

At first glance it may look as though you are escaping the ghost voices of your childhood. More often, by avoiding your parents' choices all you are doing is limiting your own. Once again, this kind of programming tends to make us superficial in a way that works against our best interests.

Programmed for Limited Communication

My friend Sam says that nobody in his family knew how to express their feelings. When his mother got angry, she closed down and stopped talking—sometimes for days; when his father got angry, he yelled, slammed doors, and then stormed out of the house. To this day, Sam says that arguments terrify him. The slightest disagreements can feel like the end of the world.

Each of us came from a family that had its own style of communicating. Some families didn't talk about sex, for example; other families didn't talk about anything but sex. Some families talked about politics; other families talked about feelings. Some families consistently gave encouraging words of support; some families specialized in criticism and the cold water treatment. Some families didn't talk; and some families screamed. My friend Courtney has two brothers. She says that in her family, she, one brother, and her father are steady-stream talkers. Her mother and one brother are basically very quiet. One group was always talking; the other was always listening. Years later, her quiet brother told her that he resented never being able to get a word in edgewise. As an adult, he married a woman who talks even less than he does, and she is now threatening divorce, saying that as a couple they never communicate.

It's hard work to break the communicating programs that were instilled in us as children. But we can do it. We can become aware of how we communicate; we can learn to listen; we can learn to be caring in our words and tone; and we can encourage our loved ones to do the same. It all starts by becoming aware of our programming.

Programmed to Be Comfortable With Conflict

Madeleine is dating a man whom she describes as sensitive, kind, supportive, and thoughtful. So what's wrong? Madeleine feels bored. Even though they have a great deal in common and a wonderful sex life, Madeleine doesn't feel stimulated. She finds herself picking arguments and causing dissension. She's concerned that her partner could become "fed-up" with her bickering and leave her.

Because of this she went into therapy. It didn't take her therapist many sessions to bring something major to her attention. Madeleine is a middle child with two older and two younger brothers. Growing up, the five siblings were very confrontational with each other. In fact, Madeleine often felt picked on, and she hated it. Nonetheless, the combative relationship she and her siblings shared became her model for how relationships should feel. She is accustomed to living in an environment where two people communicate by looking for trouble. One says, "You left something rotten in the fridge." The other says, "Did not." "Did so," comes the reply. "You're a dummy." "Am not." "Are so." No matter where Madeleine goes, in her head her siblings are never far away.

Programmed to Create Crisis

Some of us have been programmed for drama. If it's missing, we feel bored, empty, and edgy. We use drama to bring back the early experiences of family; we use drama to make us feel more alive; we use dramas to give us projects; we use drama to keep ourselves from doing what we should be doing; we use drama to get attention and to test our partners; and we use drama as a way of avoiding the real life that happens when drama stops.

There are dozens of ways to find trouble. You can create your own situations or you can embrace someone else's drama as though it were your own. How does this programming affect your relationships?

- You may choose people who are always in trouble—people with addictions; people with financial or emotional problems; people who are involved in ongoing struggles; people who pull you into their maelstroms.
- You may frighten away people who don't like drama.
- You may find yourself using crisis as a substitute for intimacy.

It's certainly true that people can grow closer by surviving a critical experience together. Crisis, however, should never become the foundation of a relationship.

Programmed to Choose Unavailable Partners

"Why do commitmentphobic men/women always find me? Why do I find them?" So many people have asked me this question, and I always have essentially the same answer. We choose unavailable partners—people who live in other countries or states, already have primary relationships, or are blatantly commitmentphobic—because we are comfortable with the way these relationships make us feel. In some ways, they are familiar. Something in our life experiences programmed us to distrust closeness and, conversely, to become accustomed to relationships that were distant.

When I ran relationship workshops about commitmentphobia, many of the female participants described emotionally unavailable fathers—fathers who worked long hours, fathers who related in grunts and sign language, fathers who ran hot and cold, fathers who didn't live at home, and even fathers who were essentially loving but didn't know how to communicate their feelings. These paternal relationships created a sense of longing in these women, which they have unwittingly carried forward into their adult lives.

Of course, you can do something different; you can find partners who are present and available for you. But you can only do this if you are very aware of your tendencies, and very determined to stay awake in your relationships. It all begins with the people you choose. This is one of the reasons why I tell those who have a tendency to get involved in relationships I call commitmentphobic to find out as much as they possibly can about a potential partner's history *before* they get involved. This is one of my broken record–type speeches, but that doesn't make it any less important.

Programmed to Pull Back When Someone Gets Too Close

Were you programmed to believe that all love is "smothering love" or guilt-provoking love? Did you have domineering or over-protective caregivers? Did you have parents whose love came with so many demands or so much abuse that you withdrew from love itself?

My friend James, for example, cringes anytime someone does something nice for him. He doesn't ever want his girlfriend to buy him presents, cook him a meal, or help him do anything. Instead of seeing these things as caring tokens of her love, he experiences them as a set up for future demands and future guilt. He says that his mother's love came with yards and yards of tangled, convoluted strings. Yes he wants a relationship, but on his terms. He doesn't want to take, and he doesn't want to give so much that he feels engulfed by someone else's needs. James needs to begin to work on ways of reprogramming himself, one step at a time. Recently James and his girlfriend started seeing a couples' counselor, and they are both finding it very helpful.

Programmed to Stay When You Should Leave

"Why Am I Putting Up With Such Abuse?" I've had far too many serious conversations with men and women who ask themselves that question. There is usually at least one common theme: Whether the abuse is physical or emotional, all of these men and women seem to think that they can "handle" what is taking place. They feel as though they have survived similar or even worse experiences, and therefore believe they can survive it again. In short, some other experience has programmed them to tolerate behavior that shouldn't be tolerated. Often these people react very differently if they see someone else being treated as they are being treated. If you are in an abusive relationship, ask yourself how you would feel if you saw a loved one being treated as you are being treated. How would you advise that loved one?

Programmed to Leave When You Should Stay

Have you ever had the experience of really liking, trusting, and being attracted to someone, but still wanting to move on? Some of us are programmed to never get our feet wet. We always make sure we have a "way out"—a little window through which we can exit the relationship, should it ever become necessary. We still believe that maybe, just maybe, there will be somebody who is cuter, thinner, smarter, sexier, less demanding, more communicative.

When Ghost Programs Collide

It's been my experience that the greatest commitment problems arise for those of us who carry two separate and distinct ghost programs that are in direct conflict with each other. This sounds complicated, so let me give you some examples to make the picture clear.

Tasha's earliest experiences gave her no good role models for a loving relationship. In fact her family was so dysfunctional that she always felt "different" from everyone else. She didn't want to date the guy next door type because she didn't believe guys like this could appreciate her. She didn't want to be part of a suburban couple because she saw that lifestyle as a hypocritical facade. But Tasha's rich imagination compensated for her early disappointments by helping her develop a powerful fantasy program to substitute for the loving relationships she could not find. In these fantasies, Tasha would somehow meet a brilliant, sensitive man who would "understand" her, as she "understood him." Ordinary life wasn't good enough for her, and neither was an ordinary partner. Her fantasy program told her that she deserved a "charmed" life, a larger-than-life life, with a larger-than-life partner who would confirm her "specialness."

When Tasha meets a man, her two programs collide. On the one hand, she immediately rejects any man who looks too "normal"— any man who offers real possibility for relationship. On the other hand, she latches on to the messages she receives from men with powerful seduction techniques, paying little or no attention to the reality of what they are saying. She doesn't notice whether these men are stable, faithful, or sincere. She doesn't even always notice whether these men have other girlfriends or even wives. She doesn't notice that these men have no history of commitment. And then she is shattered when she can't get them to commit to her.

Alex's programs are also on a constant collision course with each other. Alex's earliest years left him with an enormous void in his life that is always crying out to be filled. You could say that he has been programmed to be needy. At the same time, he has another program that he developed to compensate for what was missing in his life. This is Alex's "free as a bird" program. He wants to be free of attachments, able to start a new and exciting life with only a moment's notice.

When Alex meets a woman he is attracted to, the first thing that gets activated is his need. So in the beginning of a relationship, he will do anything and everything to make a deep heart connection. But soon Alex's profound neediness comes into direct conflict with his fantasy need—the need to be unchained. And the results of this conflict are completely confusing to any woman who lets herself get close to him. Late at night, or early in the morning, Alex is a love-starved snuggle bunny who can't get enough affection. But as the day wears on, Alex starts thinking of airports. And he sees himself going *alone*. Dr. Jekyll at one moment, Mr. Hyde the next. This cannot be easy for Alex. But think about how his partners feel.

As you can see from these two examples, conflicting programs can have their origins in the same set of circumstances. But whatever the origins of the programs, the end result is trouble. Conflicting programs lead to damaging circumstances. Someone is always getting hurt. And most of the time, everyone is getting hurt.

How Fantasy Programs and Commitment Issues Come Together

Our dreams give us inspiration, goals, and hopes. They can even help heal our injuries. This is certainly true even for romantic fantasies and dreams. But fantasies need to be kept in their place with a regular dose of healthy reality. Without an appropriate sense of balance, fantasies can confuse us, create a profound sense of longing, and steer us further and further away from concrete real possibilities. And this is a setup for trouble.

When someone who has grown up in the absence of good relationship role models turns to fantasy to fulfill his or her needs, there is a tendency to close the door on real partnerships and instead focus on our dream lovers. Many men and women will accept nothing less than idealized love. They wait for it to come. Too often what they find instead of love is someone with a truly superb capacity to weave stories that mesh with our fantasies.

When a man or women who has grown up with no sound sense of what a real relationship should feel like meets a potential partner who is "selling" hardcore romantic fantasies, the dysfunctional relationship program collides with the hopeful fantasy program, and the mix can be incredibly hurtful. Our hearts open instantaneously, without asking questions, without taking precautions, certain that the search is over. However fantasy partners have little interest in delivering reality, and they resent it if you have the courage to ask. Fantasy partners live in fantasy too. They aren't interested in settling down; they aren't interested in building a life; and they aren't interested in talking about it with you in therapy. Their only interest is their own pursuit of fantasy.

There will always be men and women who peddle fantasy— people trying to sell you dreams without a delivery date. So the buyer must beware. Understanding the flawed alchemy of fantasy programming is your own best defense against whatever deficits may exist in your relationship software. This understanding will protect you from the damaging potential of other people's fantasies, but perhaps even more important, it will protect you from your own.

Getting in Touch with Your Own Programming

We all know people who are victims of their programming. It's so obvious when we look at the people around us: Programming is Carl needing a woman he can boss around and then rejecting her because she lets him. Programming is Richard marrying one woman with drug problems, one women with alcohol problems, and one woman whose alcoholic relatives dominate their home life. Programming is Bobbie dating resumés instead of people. What are your programs?

What we need to recognize is that all of these programs bring us to the same destination: A place of being very far away from a lasting intimate connection we can truly trust. Whether we have been programmed to (a) enjoy distance—by sitting home with our computers, our romantic novels, and our user-friendly television sets; or (b) accept distance—by putting up with partners who don't want intimacy, the end result is still distance. And distance is the antithesis of meaningful connection. Meaningful connection happens when two individuals come *together* over and over, in an atmosphere of trust and openness and vulnerability—without fantasy, crisis, or any abusive behavior.

All of us grow comfortable with our ghosts; we get used to the legacy of programming that these ghosts have provided. Like it or not, it feels like "who we are." And it's hard to imagine feeling differently. It's easy to accept our programming and feel sorry for ourselves for being dealt such a difficult hand. When we do that our ghosts harden inside of us, making change more and more of a challenge.

> It takes courage to challenge the ghost programs that are running your relationships

It takes enormous courage to look your ghosts in the eye and examine your programming. It takes courage to challenge the ghost programs that are running your relationships. (Did I say ruining, because it's what I'm thinking.) Liberation starts by committing yourself to reprogramming yourself, one program at a time.

I know how difficult it is. I knew my wife for six months before we had a date. I didn't think she was my type. After our second date, all the negative programs in my head started to run fighting against the possibility of love. I became terrified. This is all wrong I screamed, to myself. She's too short. I'm too tall. I don't know if I'm really ready to grow up. I knew I had met someone who offered the possibility of a relationship that deserved the hard work every relationship entails. But knowing what I know I still responded with all my negative programming. On our third date, there was a crisis, a serious misunderstanding; I saw my out, and I took it. I gave her a long speech about why I just couldn't move forward. I went home and realized the magnitude of the mistake I had just made. I called my therapist. I called several friends. I called Jill. After that, I've never looked back. But many times I had to struggle against my ghostlike fears and programming.

I learned, and you can too, that these programs are not carved in stone—unless of course you choose them to be. Yes, you can spend the rest of your life embracing your ghosts, embracing your programming, and feeling sorry for yourself for being dealt such a difficult hand. Or you can commit yourself right here and now to setting yourself free, step-by-step, one ghost at a time.

Releasing your ghosts and peeling off the layers of programming can feel like a daunting task. But the payoff is found in connections that feel real and continue to build from there. Will you be lost without your lifelong ghostly companions? I believe you will be *found* because as the ghosts and their programs slowly dissolve, what is left is a more authentic you. And that "you" is a person who will be better at loving than any ghost or program could ever be.

The Courage to Find and Fight for the Self

*L*ong before I ever had the experience or the tools to understand what it meant, I would hear people say that you have to have a commitment to yourself before you can make a commitment to another person. That you have to care about yourself before you can care about another person. That you have to be able to be alone before you can be in a loving relationship. That you have to have a life of your own before you can truly build and share a life with another person. You too have probably heard lines like these dozens of times. You may have even given such advice to friends.

I know that a lot of people who are reading this right now are thinking, "I'm alone all the time. Too much of the time, in fact. I know how to be alone." Or you're thinking, "I have a life, I just want to find someone I can share it with." Or you're thinking, "I have a relationship with myself, I want a relationship with a partner." Yet I also know that these very same people are also *waiting* for "real" life to begin, the life that includes a loving relationship. There is nothing wrong with hoping for lasting love in your life. But this hope also has a way of undermining the possibility of actually finding it.

Part of the process of making yourself "ready" for partnership is building a caring relationship with yourself and creating a fulfilling life. Not a temporary life that will "do" until the magical "he" or "she" comes along. But a life you are committed to—so committed to that you would find yourself hard pressed to make radical changes. Think about what it means to have a balanced life that you value and that makes you feel good and complete, with or without a partner.

I remember that *three days* before I met my wife I said to my therapist, "I like my life the way it is right now. I'm not sure where a relationship would fit into it. It would take a lot of accommodating, and I don't know if that's something I want to do. Maybe I'm supposed to be single." As strange as my words may sound to you (I must say that they sounded pretty strange to me too), that very feeling of contentment was the thing that tipped the scales in my favor. It was the thing that actually enabled my life to open up. It was the thing that enabled me to find a healthy partner. Because having a life that you care about and are committed to is the secret ingredient to building a larger life—a life with a loving partner—that you also care about and are committed to.

Here are some questions to think about:

- If you don't have a loving relationship with yourself—if you have little regard for who you are as a person and your value as a human being—how can you begin to make a loving commitment to someone else?
- If you lose your connection to yourself in relationships—lose sight of your needs, your values, your priorities, your goals—how can you maintain a loving connection to someone else?
- If you don't even know who you really are—if your truest self remains a mystery to you—how can you successfully connect with and stay committed to another person?

These are some of the most fundamental questions of the "self." And their implications regarding your ability or inability to find and stay in a committed relationship can be enormous.

This challenge to commitment is not just about the importance of self-esteem. Don't get me wrong. There is no arguing, certainly not from me, that the issue of self-esteem is one of the important undercurrents in the commitmentphobic struggle. But self-esteem is only one of many "issues of the self" that can impact dramatically on commitment fears and fantasies. There is a bigger picture that you don't want to miss. And we need to look at this larger picture first.

Talking About the Self / Talking About Connection

When we talk about the "self," and how it affects our ability to connect and stay connected in relationship, there are actually three different areas of vulnerability:

LOW SELF-ESTEEM

LOSS OF SELF

LACK OF SELF

Let's start with a short summary of each.

Low Self-Esteem: Most of us struggle with issues of our own self-worth. Negative voices swirl in our heads, leading us to a host of self-defeating behaviors. And in the arena of relationships, these voices tend to be particularly loud. Do you struggle with low self-esteem: Do you put your partners on a pedestal, but often devalue yourself? If something goes wrong, do you always think it's your fault? Are you always waiting to get the negative outcome you "deserve"? Are you your own worst critic? Are you unnecessarily critical of others to compensate for your own self-doubts? Are you always questioning your judgments, your decisions, and your choices? Do you tend to "settle" for less in life because you don't fully believe you deserve more? Do you give too much because it's the only way you believe you can get what you want? Do you brag excessively to make yourself look more attractive? These are all symptoms of low self-esteem.

Loss of Self: Are you one of those people who loses your *self* in a relationship? Loses your boundaries? Loses your priorities? Loses sight of your needs? Loses sight of your values? Or all of the above. If this is your issue, you probably know what I'm talking about, since your struggle to stay in a relationship is particularly painful. Do you have an impossible time holding on to you in the presence of a strong partner? Do you become "a different person"—a person you don't really know or like? Do your boundaries blur? Do you feel engulfed? Do you give away the store (give up more than you can afford) in an attempt to be loved? Your biggest battle in a relationship is the battle to hold on to yourself. And it's a battle you are constantly losing.

Lack of Self: Who are you? What is important to you? What are your values? What are your strengths? What do you bring to a relationship? What do you need from a relationship? For some people, there are no firm answers to these questions. Many of us, even though we are fully grown adults, are still working from a very poorly defined sense of who we are. Often, we function from a false persona—a face we "put on" to meet the world that lacks a genuine sense of connection to our souls. Do you look to your relationship to define you in the world? Are you angry when it does not fulfill that function? Do you feel lost when you don't have love in your life? Are you constantly disappointed by your partners' inability to keep your relationships feeling magical? Does your life, in general, feel disconnected? These various expressions of "hollowness" inside point to a lack of a well-defined self.

Let's now take a closer look at these three separate and distinct issues of the "self." It is so very important to understand how each affects our choices, our behaviors, our fears, and our overall ability to function in a relationship.

#1 Issue of the Self: Low Self-Esteem

"Isn't the fear of commitment really just a reflection of underlying issues of self esteem?" Every single time I have ever given a talk about commitment and commitmentphobia there has been at least one person in the room—speaking, no doubt, for many—who has posed this question. Sometimes, the person asking this question is thinking to herself/himself, "Isn't my partner's commitment problem really a self-esteem problem?" Other times, they are thinking exactly the opposite, i.e., "Isn't the reason I am *attracted to* people with commitment problems due to *my* own lack of self-esteem?"

Self-esteem is one of the most powerful catch phrases of our times and it tends to get used as a "diagnosis" for many, if not most, of our relationship ills. So it shouldn't come as much of a surprise that people would love to use the concept of self-esteem to explain away the phenomenon we call commitment fear. It would be lovely if we could label every commitment problem a self-esteem problem and package this complex phenomenon into something so straightforward and simple. Unfortunately, the commitment problem is not all that simple. And you have already seen many examples that clearly contradict this "globalized" assumption. The very fact that people can *use* the self-esteem label to *escape* responsibility for their commitment conflicts just as easily as they can use it to *assume* too much responsibility for the very same conflicts, illustrates how poorly the relationship between low self-esteem and commitment conflict is really understood.

the commitment problem is not all that simple

Still, these people are not altogether wrong in their thinking. *Sometimes*, low self-esteem is at the heart of the struggle to connect. *Sometimes*, low self-esteem is the "thing" that is driving people's fear. *Sometimes* low self-esteem is the force that leads us to all the wrong choices. And these are some of the scenarios we need to examine now.

Alicia: The Classic "Low Self-Esteem" Story

Every time I give a workshop or talk I will meet at least two or three women like Alicia. Alicia feels as though she has been victimized by almost every relationship she has ever been in. And the setup always seems to be the same. Every relationship starts with a strong pursuit, and Alicia, even if she is hesitant at first, always feels grateful to be chosen. These men always seem to "find" her, since she does little to actively seek connection. And they also seem to want her so much— at least in the beginning.

Once she has been "chosen," Alicia's guard is easily worn down by the apparent sincerity of her suitor. The prevailing emotion at the time is, "I can't believe he wants *me*." But then typically at some point in the relationship her suitor has an unexpected and unexplained change of heart, and pursuit turns to panic. This always leaves Alicia angry and confused, particularly since "he was the one who pushed for closeness."

Alicia doesn't believe she has a lot of choices when it comes to love. She believes she has to wait patiently and make the best of what comes her way. She doesn't feel she can be too picky, she doesn't feel she can be too difficult, she doesn't feel she has any power to choose the people she is interested in. When someone does find her, part of her always feels it is her last chance. And she has accepted this position of powerlessness.

Alicia has actually had five "last chances" in the past three years. But her belief system never changes. And her behavior never changes. And her "gratefulness" never changes. Because her low self-esteem is the loudest voice in her head.

Karlin: A Woman Who Tries to "Play It Safe"

Karlin is one of the brightest, most interesting, multi-talented women you are ever likely to meet in the city of Los Angeles. And that is saying a lot. She is a gifted actress, an accomplished writer, a concerned political activist, and she gives dinner parties that make you think that Martha Stewart is hiding out in the kitchen.

Karlin's list of friends reads like a Who's Who of people you'd like to spend more time with. But Karlin's list of ex-boyfriends reads like a Who's Who of deadbeats, misfits, and going-nowhere-fasts. If he doesn't have a job, Karlin has probably dated him. If he doesn't have two nickels to rub together, Karlin has probably dated him. And if he has a short criminal record, Karlin almost married him.

All of Karlin's friends, who love her dearly, look at Karlin and ask themselves "Why?" And so does Karlin. Karlin knows she deserves more. Karlin knows she has more to offer. But she always winds up with men who she believes will be "safe." Karlin's definition of safe is a man who is in awe of her, a man who puts her on a pedestal, and a man who feels inferior to her. Karlin believes that men like this will be less likely to reject her, which, by the way, is not always true.

Karlin is never happy in the relationships she chooses. She is always aware that her various beaus are not the people she would like them to be. She is always frustrated that her relationships lack depth, always disappointed that she doesn't have more. To herself and a few of her closest friends, Karlin acknowledges that her various boyfriends have left much to be desired...Yet she keeps choosing different variations of the exact same theme. Karlin is terrified of reaching for more, but always angry that she has settled for less. It's a Catch-22 that keeps her out of committed relationships, and it is driven by her lack of self-esteem.

Maria: A Different Kind of Story, But the Ending Is the Same

Maria knows exactly who she is. Her personality is well defined. Her temperament is well defined. Her values are well defined. Her likes and dislikes are well defined. Her needs are well defined. When she is home alone or with her best friends, Maria is smart, wickedly funny and sarcastic, a little bit opinionated, eccentric, and fun to be with. There's only one problem: this is not the Maria whom she presents to the world.

Out in the world—at work, at school, on dates—Maria labors to be "perfect." She works incredibly hard to present to people the Maria she thinks they want: the sweet Maria, the charming Maria, the understanding Maria, the always upbeat Maria. Not surprisingly, Maria has a lot of superficial friendships. But also not surprisingly, these friendships never go anywhere.

Why does Maria act this way? Low self-esteem. Maria is always performing because she feels that the real Maria would not be welcome and would not be liked. This is clearly a self-esteem conflict. Fearing rejection, unwilling to take risks, and believing that her genuine self is not valuable, Maria chooses to play it safe and trot out the "edited" Maria.

In intimate relationships, this backfires in all kinds of ways. One way or the other, Maria doesn't let herself be known. Either she is running away from men who are interested in getting to know her, or gravitating toward men who have no interest in who she really is. Either way, Maria ends up feeling alone. While there is a part of Maria that *craves* a relationship, the more powerful voice inside of Maria wants to be left alone. That's because she is so terrified of being revealed, and scared that the real Maria would never be accepted or loved.

Edward: A Fourth Variation, But Again the Same Ending

Edward has had a long, painful history of relationships gone bust. His first wife left him for another man. His second wife left him for another woman. And he's just waiting for his third wife to tell him to start packing. Every time Edward talks about his wife, he always starts with a comment such as, "I don't know what she sees in me" or "I still don't know why she married *me*." His internal dialogue is even worse. To himself he is saying, "She married me because I have money" or "She married me because she was scared of being alone" or "She married me because I got her pregnant."

Edward has never been able to trust a single woman he has been with. But a large part of this is due to the way he sets the relationships up. Because he feels he has little value as a human being, Edward does everything he can to sell women on his value as a husband. He has always driven incredibly expensive cars that are easily "noticed," and he has always spent excessively when he dates. If he is dating a woman he likes, he immediately starts offering to help pay her bills. Before long, he has moved her into his house, without ever asking for any help with his expenses.

Edward never tries to make an emotional connection first. He always connects first through money. He purchases attention and affection before he ever gets a chance to see whether or not he could receive them because he is a decent human being deserving of love. Then he spends the duration of each relationship feeling distrustful and closed off, wondering if his partner really cares about him at all. Most of these relationships don't last very long. But even the ones that do last never feel genuinely intimate and loving.

As you might imagine, Edward's setup has ended in predictable results. When his first wife left him, she took him to the cleaners. His second wife left with her share of his income too. When his third wife refused to sign a prenuptial agreement,

Edward immediately concluded that she had plans to ultimately exit. He sits in fear of that day.

Edward can't really afford to conduct his relationships this way. He can't afford it financially, and, more importantly, he can't afford it emotionally. As each relationship passes, he becomes more and more bitter. More and more cynical. More and more distrusting. Edward has finally reached the point where he doesn't even *want* to conduct his relationships in this way. He is just too terrified to try to do it any differently.

Alicia, Maria, Anna, and Edward are very different people, but they have two important things in common. They all suffer from low self-esteem. And they all keep ending up alone, from a mechanism that is fueled by their low self-esteem.

How might your issues with self-esteem be affecting your ability to make and keep a meaningful emotional connection? Do you see yourself in any of these stories?

Breaking the Low Self-Esteem Cycle

Every single one of us is deserving of love, but reaching that conclusion for yourself may require some work. Low self-esteem is a terrible burden. It beats you up over and over again, leaving you more and more convinced that just being who you are is never enough. Yet low self-esteem does not have to be a life sentence. We see, hear, and read about "success" stories every day. There's only one catch: only *you* can take the steps required to break its vicious cycle.

When we are young, negative voices from parents, other family, peers, teachers, etc. make us feel we are not worthy of love. Or that our worth is conditional. And these voices are often reinforced with negative experiences. But when we grow up, those voices become our own voice. We become our own worst critic. Even if our original critics have long since disappeared from our lives. This is why change begins with you.

This is also why the struggle to build self-esteem often starts in the mirror, learning to say loving words to yourself, and giving yourself praise. The goal is to create a new internal voice that speaks louder and more clearly than the old destructive ones. Simple, yes, but also very powerful.

Building self-esteem also means surrounding yourself with people who speak to you with supportive and loving voices; it means walking away from people who are hurtful and negative. You probably have friends, and peers, and family members who still fill your ears with negativity—external voices you continue to tolerate. If these people can't change the voices they bring to you, you must change the nature of these relationships. Creating distance can be a very self-loving act when it hurts too much to stay close.

Building self-esteem means taking risks—risking to be accepted or rejected for who you really are, not for what you can do or give. Are you willing to take these risks? Perhaps you are more willing today than you have ever been before, now that you see how little you have to lose.

Low Self-Esteem Lowers Your Chances of Finding and Making a Committed Connection

Perhaps the most important thing you can do for yourself right now, is allow yourself to see a complete picture of how a lack of self-esteem can rule your life and sabotage your prospects for commitment and connection.

Low self-esteem...

...leads to bad choices.

Instead of actively looking for partners who have the characteristics you desire, and rejecting those who don't measure up to a reasonable set of expectations, you are always "thrilled" when *anyone* chooses you. But these "anyones" rarely, if ever, deliver a committed relationship.

... makes you unnecessarily grateful.

Instead of struggling to build your relationship into something more rewarding, just *having* a relationship is enough. You want commitment and a deeper connection, but you would never press for it.

... stops you from asking the hard questions.

If you genuinely don't believe you are worthy, you're going to have a hard time asking a potential partner the hard questions: Questions about fidelity, love, children, abusive behavior, addictive patterns, the person your *partner* is still married to! Low self-esteem stops you from rocking the boat. But these are the questions that clear the way for commitment.

... inhibits you from standing up for your needs.

You convince yourself that your needs are not important and that everyone else's needs come first. As a result, you are devalued and not taken seriously. Of course this makes you bitter, while also sabotaging your capacity to connect.

... lets you put other people on a pedestal.

They are everything, you are nothing. At least that's how your attitude comes across. This leads people to take you for granted, and to have little appreciation for how special *you* are. As a result, you are never considered a worthy partner for commitment.

... keeps you from taking emotional risks.

Making a deeper connection with another human being *demands* that you take emotional risks and reveal who you are. Sharing feelings, sharing fears, sharing secrets, sharing the real you. If you won't take the risks, you don't get the connection.

... makes you want to play it safe.

But haven't you learned by now that there is no such thing as playing it safe in relationships? Whether you only make "safe" choices, or you exhibit only "safe" behaviors, if you're not getting what you deserve, you're going to be unhappy and unfulfilled. Even if the prospect for commitment arises, either you can't value it or you can't trust it.

. . . often makes you overly critical of others.

Many of us compensate for our own feelings of low worth by taking down others until they reach our level. "She's not pretty enough." "He's not smart enough." "She has a bad job." "He has bad skin." You find something wrong with almost everyone, and you embrace their faults because it makes you feel more desirable. But this backfires when you try to make emotional bonds. Being overly critical of others drives decent people away. And you often find yourself trying to negotiate a relationship with someone who intimidates you, or who is dangerously narcissistic, because these are the only people who "pass" your rigid evaluations. This leaves little possibility of healthy, well-intentioned commitment.

. . . lets you compensate by inflating your picture of yourself.

All you do is talk about how terrific you are. Or maybe you're a "name dropper" who never stops trying to impress people with who you know. You think this is going to make people like you, but it tends to have the opposite effect, encouraging most people to keep their distance. Only the people who buy your stories are likely to stick around, yet you tend to be contemptuous of their gullibility, seeing them as unworthy of serious commitment.

#2 ISSUE OF THE SELF: LOSS OF SELF

What exactly are we losing when we "lose our selves" in a relationship? That depends on who you are. Some of us lose our confidence, our strength and independence, or our sense of self-control. Some of us lose our judgment and the sense of balance in our lives. But many of us lose the connection to our fundamental core. And these lost connections cost us dearly when it comes to love. Do any of the following variations on this theme sound familiar?

When You Are in a Relationship . . .

. . . do you lose your boundaries?

Corinna does. Corinna is a '90s woman. She is strong, tough, opinionated, fiercely independent. Until she meets a man who turns her on. Then in a heartbeat, everything changes. Mi casa becomes su casa. What's mine is yours, and hopefully, vice versa. Use my phone. Eat my food. Borrow my money. Move on in! And it's not just about physical boundaries. For Corinna, all the lines get blurry. A partner's victories become her victories, a partner's joys become her joys. But a partner's failures also become her failures. A partner's problems become her problems. Corinna can't hold on to her boundaries. And it scares the men she loves. Is your inability to keep firm boundaries scaring away the man or woman *you* love?

. . . do you lose sight of priorities?

When you're in a relationship, does everything else—friendships, family, work, goals—get put on the back burner? Does the relationship become *everything*? Do you give up the life you had to become immersed in a potential new life? If so, you are asking your partner to deliver you an entire world. Talk about pressure! And to add insult to injury, when this strategy backfires, you are often left with less than you came in with.

. . . do you lose sight of your needs?

That's what happens to people who lose too much of themselves in a relationship. Instead of attending to a clearly defined set of needs, such a person's attitude becomes, "I'll take whatever you've got." "I need a partner who is monogamous" becomes "I can wait for him/her to change." "I need a partner who can talk about feelings" becomes "I can find someone else for that." "I need a partner who can share expenses with me" becomes, "I make enough for both of us." But settling for less doesn't mean that you are going to be happy with less. And feelings of discontent inevitably create powerful rifts in your ability to feel connected to your partner.

...do you lose sight of your values?

Dan has very strong feelings about the practice of egalitarian ideas in relationship. He has always believed in sharing the work and sharing the bills. He's never looked for a free ride, and he's never wanted to carry someone else. And he's always been able to express these views openly and non-defensively to friends. But every time he meets a woman he is attracted to, Dan loses his ability to practice what he preaches. His experience with Janice is a perfect example. Janice was a self-proclaimed "princess" of the highest order, and from the moment they met, Dan opened his wallet and started to pay for everything. It started with dates and movies and small expenses. But then it graduated to automobile repairs, wardrobe, and ultimately, rent. Dan does this because he thinks he's "supposed to." Problem is, Dan resents this like hell, and feels completely boxed into an intolerable situation of his own creation. And he also loses the respect of his partner. What's the lesson? Losing sight of our values leads us to connections with little or no value.

Dan's friend Alan has very strong feelings about the dangers of heavy drinking and drug use. He also has very strong opinions about people who are drawn to these behaviors. But the moment Louisa showed up drunk on their third date, Alan became confused. And when she told him about her "misadventures" with quaaludes, his head started to spin. Red flags were waving and alarms were buzzing. But Louisa was *gorgeous,* with the kind of looks Alan had only dreamed of before. And she genuinely seem to be attracted to him. So Alan decided he could "work with it." He would try to understand the drug use, even as the stories piled up high. And he even started stocking his freezer with an ample supply of vodka. The problem is, Alan *can't* work with it. And now he knows it must end.

. . . do you lose sight of your goals?

Diana is a gifted artist slowly building her career in New York City. Art is her passion and her greatest love, and her reputation is growing. It is the place where she is most committed. Until she meets a man. Then inevitably, *his* goals become the important goals, and Diana is ready to commit herself full time to someone else's pursuit of success and put all of her aspirations on the back burner. But important goals left too long on the back burner have a way of getting overcooked and setting the kitchen on fire. Diana is always angry, though she isn't sure why. She's angry at the men in her life, and she's angry at herself. Maybe it's because her partners don't support *her* goals—or don't even ask if she has any. Or maybe it's because *she* doesn't support her own goals, and is always left feeling cheated.

. . . do you completely lose sight of who you are?

You say that you loathe cold weather, but you're learning to ski to be with someone you love. You say that you're a strict vegetarian, but you find yourself roasting a pig to please someone you love. You say that you're a musician, but you commit yourself to a corporate track to please the one you love. You say that you're a committed Democrat, but you find yourself hosting a Republican fund-raiser to support the political passions of the one you love. And for a while, you're okay with these radical departures. But an internal sense of discomfort, disappointment, and yes, even resentment, grows inside of you. In the beginning, you can manage it. But it grows larger, and your constant sense of frustration leads to depression or fury. Meanwhile, your partners are always taking your malleability for granted, and often taking advantage of it. Over time, your sense of connection disintegrates.

Losing the Self Loses the Commitment Connection

When we lose ourselves in relationship, the outcome is rarely positive. The typical result is usually some combination of bitterness, frustration, alienation, anger, and depression. You end up with people who don't appreciate you; you end up with people who take you for granted; you end up with people who don't have a clue about what intimacy means. Not exactly the key ingredients to a committed partnership. At best, this is disorienting. At worst, it is painful, costly, and self-destructive. And it is always disconnecting.

People who lose themselves in a relationship ultimately become fearful of committing, and understandably so. Their experiences have shown them that they lose too much every time they love, and they have been worn down by the losses. What these people need to understand is that their primary commitment must be a commitment to honoring the self. To championing the self. To fighting tooth and nail for every shred of self. No matter what it takes; no matter what others think, say, or do; no matter how tough the fight; it is the only road worth taking. This is not selfish. And it is not self-destructive. It is healthy and necessary if you hope to build a meaningful and rewarding connection.

#3 ISSUE OF SELF: LACK OF SELF

Each of us is born with the seeds of a self, seeds that have the potential to develop into a full and powerful, unique self. But the experience of childhood does not always support this "second birth." For some of us, the challenges of childhood obliterate those seeds, or fracture them, or restrain them from fully blossoming. Instead of being nurtured and supported with unconditional love to become the fullest expression of the individual we are, at a very early age we are forced into molds, coerced, intimidated, or even abused into following footsteps that are not our own. Painfully, we learn early on in life that love is completely conditional. Eager to please, and terrified of abandonment, we comply. We give away our selves in order to get love. And the internal connection to our fullest potential is buried deep underground.

This particular struggle of the self is the hardest one for most people to understand. If it isn't your struggle, it's difficult to imagine. And if it *is* your struggle, it's even harder to imagine—you've been too well programmed to ever consider that the person you present to the world is not really who you are.

Here's the part that is most confusing: those of us with a poorly defined sense of self tend to have a very well-defined "false self." This false self is an "internal impostor" that tells us who we are, and how we need to live. Instead of having a well-defined center to which we can turn *in* for guidance and answers, our head is filled with rules and regulations to which we comply. This false self may have an answer for everything — how to walk and how to talk, when to smile and when to frown, how to feel and when to feel it, right and wrong, good and bad, attitudes and opinions. These rules and regulations are a life-saver for someone who cannot access genuine feelings of self. They make survival possible. Yet deep inside, rests a nagging feeling of emptiness, an emptiness that rises to the surface when we are alone too long.

Why Love Is Never Enough (Or Always Way Too Much)

What does any of this have to do with relationships? And, for that matter, what does it have to do with commitment? The answer, actually, is a simple one. An absence of internal connections wreaks havoc on external connections (i.e., the thing we call relationship). Without a solid internal foundation, romantic relations are painfully vital as well as painfully vulnerable. You must have love to fill you up, but it never seems to be enough because there is always a hole inside—a hole that comes from an absence of self. So you are always wanting, and always trying to connect, but you are also always critical of that connection. No matter how much your partner can offer, it is never really enough. Only fantasies have the power to fill you up. Other human beings always seem to fall short. Because a lot of people can offer you love, but none can offer you a self.

And then there is the flip side.

When you don't have a well-developed sense of self, it is very easy to give away the store—you've done this all your life—but then you lash out at the person you gave it to. You don't *know* how much you are compromising until you have compromised way too much. You don't realize that you are giving away too much until you are flooded with anger over all you have given. You can be an incredibly understanding partner, until it registers somewhere deep inside you that this is not who you are.

> **You don't know how much you are compromising until you have compromised way too much.**

You can be an incredibly supportive partner, until it registers deep inside you that this is not who you are. You can be a compliant partner, until it registers deep inside you that this is not who you are. You can be a selfless partner, until it registers deep inside you that this is not who you are. You can be a fantasy partner, until it registers deep inside of you that this is not who you are. You can play all kinds of roles for a while. The only problem is that the roles can't last. Because the only "role" that is genuine is that role that is your true self.

People who suffer from a lack of authentic self can experience life as a series of acting jobs. You think that "being a partner" means you need to be a certain way, so you eagerly assume that role. And for a while, you give the performance of your life. But as you get further and further from who you really are, your internal discomfort grows. Until a tiny voice deep inside you that is the remains of your *true self* finally cries out to be heard. Perhaps you have heard the cry. It often sounds like this: "I can't stay in this relationship!" You can try to be a different kind of partner, or a different kind of person entirely, but the voice of your true self—a voice that still lives deep inside of you—will always remind you exactly who you are and what kind of partnership you can survive and flourish in.

Jello in Search of a Mold

Men and women without a fully formed self are like Jello, able to pour themselves into any number of molds. But their favorite mold, their favorite "role" is the role of the "perfect" partner. Being a perfect partner is no easy task for most "normal" people to accomplish, but it is a role well-suited for the man or woman who lacks a clearly defined self. Being a perfect partner means giving up the self, a task that comes easily when the self is so poorly defined. Being a perfect partner means being able to merge with another, and this ability to merge is a false-self trademark. These people have an uncanny ability to read other people's minds, and give them exactly what they want. They hear and see everything when they interact with a partner—every detail and nuance. They are perfectly attuned. They anticipate everything. And they attend to everything selflessly and seamlessly.

Because the recipient of this attention feels so completely "seen" and understood, the bond this creates is unique. If you've ever felt this bond, you have probably never forgotten it. It feels as though you have made a karmic connection, that you have finally found your soul mate.

And this connection holds extraordinary power, making it easy to fall in love. But literally overnight, bliss can turn to shock, as your karmic partner suddenly rebels. The he or she that seemed perfectly content with your absolutely perfect union can suddenly reject you with the force of a freight train—and seem to have no guilt or remorse. The pain is staggering. It makes no sense. Your world turns upside down. And you desperately search for answers. But the explanation is really quite simple: The "giver" of all this good stuff can't keep giving. Your "perfect" partner has experienced an internal rebellion—he/she has finally heard the "internal cry." The bits and pieces of real self have suddenly attacked the false self. They can't go on pretending, they can't keep being someone they are not, and they need to smash the mold.

Without the Self, Commitment Is Terrifying

Perhaps you can now see more clearly how true commitment is improbable, if not impossible, in the absence of a self. And you can probably also see how a false-self seduction is simply a painful setup for a commitment that can not be delivered. It is my opinion that this particular struggle leads to the most painful relationship scenarios. Perfect beginnings turn into brutal endings, and perfect partners turn to dust. The prospects for commitment which once loomed so large vanish into thin air. And nothing is left but our memories. It all seems so crazy. But the explanation is a simple one. Real love can not build without the foundation of a self.

A Role I Couldn't Live With

How does someone like myself, who is not a therapist, know so much about this painful struggle? The answer is an equally painful one: this was once my struggle. I was the compliant partner. I was the fantasy partner. I was the overly attentive partner. I was the ridiculously understanding partner. I was the selflessly supportive partner. I was the "perfect" partner. I gave and gave and gave and gave until I couldn't carry on the role. And then, always in a heartbeat, I took it all away.

And it is important for me to let you as the reader know that probably the single greatest obstacle on my road to relationship recovery and commitment was finding and nurturing a true sense of self. If this is *your* struggle, health and love wait for you on the very same path. Whether it means spending more time alone, spending more time in meditation, or spending more time in therapy and/or support groups, it is worth the time and the trouble. I encourage you to do everything in your power to make that journey possible.

Strengthening the Self: Rules to Live By

- **Give up merger fantasies.** The urge to merge is a way of avoiding the process of finding, building, and strengthening your individual self. Love will create many moments of merger, but you need always to return to your self.
- **Take the time to find yourself.** This is the crucial step before you can strengthen and embrace the self. For some people, this finding process is too difficult in the context of a relationship—do you need more time alone, or even a healthy "time-out"?
- **Place greater value on you and your separateness.** All love starts with self-love. And your separateness is your strength.
- **Understand that giving up the self is a choice you once had to make. And taking it back is also a choice—a choice you can make right now.** You can feel sorry for yourself forever for having such a difficult beginning, or you can take all of that emotional energy and channel it into your own self-improvement. You do have a choice.

- **Give up your hope that someone else will do for you what you are unable to do for yourself.** Waiting for someone else to magically alter how you feel about yourself leaves you feeling powerless. But you are not powerless. The truth is that no one but you can make you whole.
- **Give up the fear of not being liked.** You can't be liked by everyone. You don't need to be liked by everyone. You don't even *want* to be liked by everyone. And the more you like yourself, the clearer that will become.
- **Learn to be alone.** The best way to learn how to be with another person is to learn how to be alone. If issues of the self have ever derailed your relationships, the kindest thing you can do for yourself, and for your potential partners, is to take more time for you.
- **Understand that if your relationship, or lack of relationship defines who you are, who you are is not well defined.** Relationships are meant to enrich your life, not to *be* your life. It's too much pressure on the relationship and too much pressure on your partner. Look inside for definition before you look outside for connection.
- **Give up blaming others for your own shortcomings.** Self-dissatisfaction often leads to finger-pointing and blame. Take responsibility for your own struggles.
- **Don't be afraid to be selfish.** Being selfish is not a bad thing when it means you are taking better care of yourself.
- **Stand up for yourself.** This is not a risk, it is an obligation (to *you*). Don't be afraid to express who you are and what you value. One of your goals in life should be to be accepted or rejected for who you truly are. That is the most that any of us could hope for.
- **Become your biggest fan.** Start being you own best friend, champion, and supporter. This is not about deluding yourself, it's about caring for yourself, and learning that you are worthy of love.

CHALLENGE FOUR

The Courage to Stay
Grounded in Reality

*T*he capacity to get swept up in fantasy is perhaps the single biggest reason why so many of us don't have committed relationships. Too often we lead much of our personal lives somewhere in fantasy land. At times we use fantasy to rewrite history or to idealize partners who are no longer in our lives. Other times we idle away our hours longing for ideal partners who are yet to come. Sometimes we are so caught up in our fantasy lives, that we don't even notice healthy opportunities for real connection.

Typically, long before a real partner comes along, we imagine how that partner will look, sound, and act. We even imagine the kind of life we will lead with our fantasy partners.

Then a real, living, breathing person appears. *Finally!*

You smile. The living, breathing person smiles. The living, breathing person seems *very* attractive. The living, breathing person seems attracted to you as well. You feel as though the heavens have smiled down at you. And so you begin to get to know each other.

When that happens in your life, what do you do? Do you stay in fantasy with your head in the clouds? Or do you plant your feet firmly on terra firma and do everything you can to stay grounded and realistic?

Think About Your Capacity for Fantasy

Sometimes when two people meet, there is little or no chemistry. In these instances, we say that the relationship never got off the ground. But often something else even more troubling occurs: The relationship has no difficulty taking off, but then it never makes it back. That's because one or both partners continue to float, held aloft by large fantasy bubbles. Consequently the relationship never returns to the real world, which finally is where our lives are played out. If you take a hard look at couples whose love has withstood the hard tests of time, you will see that their love is taking place here and now on solid ground.

Can you truthfully say that you are able to view your partners and relationships with any clarity? Are you brave enough to ask questions to find out what your partner wants from a relationship? Are you brave enough to hear real answers? Do you process and believe negative behavior or language when you see it and hear it? Or do you reshuffle the facts to suit your rich fantasy life (i.e. he's not really rejective, he's just insecure)? Are you confusing longing, or even lust, with love? Can you tell the truth—both bad and good—about what you feel or don't feel? Can you face the truth—both bad and good—about what's taking place as it takes place?

Even while in the throes of a new love with hormones dancing and surging through your body, are you able to joyfully stay attached to the real world and *in* the relationship you have found? Are you able to see reality? This is a formidable challenge that every relationship brings.

To meet this challenge, I like to advise men and women to glue at least one foot to the floor until they *know* 100 percent that a relationship is for real and is the one they want. Doing this gives us the opportunity for romance, but it also diminishes the possibility of making a major mistake. Let's all accept the fact that we can't float through our romances, expecting that the universe and others will protect us from crashing. We've been through this too many times. We can't keep going back.

Just visualize that one foot firmly attached to the floor, filled with common sense and holding back a little. Can you see it? Can you feel it? Or are you floating in that place of child-like trust and irresponsibility. Remember that child-like trust and irresponsibility is for children who have parents who can be trusted to be responsible. You are dealing with people who have needs that don't always coincide with yours. You are dealing with people who are (a) not responsible for protecting you, and (b) vulnerable themselves.

Coming Down From the Clouds

During the many years that I didn't have a solid real relationship in my life, I found that I was always actively pursuing the idea of relationship for what I imagined it would bring. I remember thinking about love, whatever I imagined that would be, as well as regular sex, an end to non-specific longing, and the hope of having a more complete life. Like most of us, I was probably the victim of too many movies and TV shows. I had fantastic fantasies of all kinds of "magical" feelings.

My fantasies often kept me from noticing or appreciating human-scale opportunities that were right in front of my face. My head was often way up in the clouds. When a potential partner crossed my admittedly distorted angle of vision, the clouds would not part. I would not make it back to the ground. What did that mean for me? Instead of appreciating relationships with women who seemed approachable, available, and genuinely nice, I would find myself creating fantasies about winning over women who were difficult, distant, and disinterested.

Those times when I did manage to find myself in a relationship with genuine potential, I never learned how to deal with what was taking place, as it was taking place. Because I expected everything to be magical and perfect, I never fully addressed major relationship issues. I never learned how to handle all the little annoyances that present themselves in a real relationship. My preferred solution to a disagreement, for example, was to shut down or think about other possible partners.

Sometimes instead of staying in the present with the woman I was with, I would find myself thinking about the ones that got away. I would focus on the significance of a memorable evening instead of moving through events as they occurred. I would think about the past, and I would be wistful. I would think about the future, and it would scare me. But my ability to be present for the day to day was practically non-existent.

Because I expected everything to be magical and perfect, I never fully addressed major relationship issues.

This tendency got me into a great deal of trouble. I would get into relationships without asking any of the right questions, I would stay in relationships hoping that problems would resolve themselves magically, and I would rarely confront difficulties as they occurred.

One of the things about my wife Jill that has impressed me almost from the first day we met is that she has never been afraid to ask the real hard questions of our relationship. She's a wonderfully romantic woman, but even so, she has always had the courage to stay grounded and deal with reality. I remember when I asked Jill to marry me, she stunned me with some very real questions. First she asked, "Why do you want to marry me?" Not a hard one to answer. I said, "Because I love you and want to be with you for the rest of my life." But that didn't seem to be enough for her because she continued to ask hard questions. "We can be together just the way things are right now... what does it mean for you to be married?

What would be different? What would be the same? How would we share responsibilities? How would we handle finances? Does this mean you want to take care of me? Does this mean you want to start a family? What does this mean for you?" That really stopped me in my tracks. I had to think about her questions and find some real answers. Frankly, I had never really gone past the romantic part, the being-together-forever-because-I-love-you part. I wasn't sure what I intended. I wasn't sure what, if anything would be different. More than anything I wanted a concrete symbol of our love. But that wasn't enough for her. She wanted to deal with reality and concrete information. She didn't want to live on hope. She wanted our relationship to be real.

Jill was very brave to ask those questions. She had to run the risk that I would think about what she asked and get scared. Instead of spinning a beautiful perfect fantasy, she made me think about things like household chores and finances. How brave of her, how self-protective, how real. It takes a great deal of courage to live in the present tense. It takes a great deal of courage to open your eyes wide and look at your relationships realistically as they are evolving.

Investing in Fantasy, Ignoring Reality

Not that long ago I had a long conversation with a woman named Theresa, who I interviewed for another book a few years back. Theresa, who is thirty-six, has been divorced for three years. About a year and a half ago, Theresa, who was working in the local library, noticed that an attractive man, also in his mid-thirties, was coming into the library every morning to read the paper.

On his way out, he would stop and chat with her for a few minutes; from these conversations she learned that he was a local businessman who owned a small company selling and servicing computer equipment. From co-workers she heard that he was one of the town's most eligible bachelors and that he "played the field." Theresa immediately began to construct pleasant fantasies featuring Patrick in the leading male role.

Two months passed before Patrick asked Theresa out. Finally one Thursday at about noon, he showed up at her desk to say that he hadn't had lunch, and would she like to join him. Then the following Thursday it happened again. It became a regular thing. He seemed so intelligent and friendly. Theresa, who was very computer literate, spent almost as much time on-line as Patrick did. She loved talking with him, but she couldn't figure out whether he was interested in her romantically, or if he thought of her as just a friend with whom he could discuss his business.

Even though Theresa really liked Patrick, she was afraid to ask him too many personal questions; she didn't want to appear pushy. Patrick offered so little personal information that she couldn't tell what was going on. Besides, someone else at the library told her that although he dated a great deal, he had one special girlfriend who lived out of town. Theresa didn't know if she could bear hearing too much about his girlfriend; she didn't want Patrick to see the hurt on her own face if he talked about another woman.

Although Theresa wasn't sure about Patrick's feelings, she was positive about her own. She had little interest in meeting anyone else, and she and her closest woman friends spent hours trying to figure out ways to get Patrick to become more romantic. Theresa even worried that despite his reputation, Patrick might be shy. Finally, after several months of lunch and conversation, Patrick told her that he was planning to open another computer store about ten miles away. He asked her if she would like to go to work for him, managing it. Theresa was thrilled. The job at the library paid very poorly, and she had been looking for something else for months. The new job would also give her a chance to get to know Patrick better.

As the opening date of the new store approached, Theresa and Patrick began to spend even more time together. He encouraged her to take some computer courses and become more knowledgeable about software and the computer industry. She found it difficult but interesting. However, despite her hopes, and even with all the time they spent together, nothing romantic happened. Patrick looked like he was interested in her, he acted like he was interested in her, but he made no effort to move the relationship along. In her heart, Theresa believed and hoped that Patrick had romantic and non-platonic feelings for her, but she had nothing concrete to pin this on. Nonetheless, Theresa felt there was an intense unspoken bond connecting the two of them. She often thought she saw it in Patrick's eyes when they looked at each other.

In the meantime, Patrick was exceptionally nice to Theresa's eight-year-old daughter Jennie, who would often come to the store with her mother. He even gave Jennie an older model computer that he no longer used, and he "souped it up" so she could use it to do homework. Theresa thought this meant that Patrick was trying to get closer to her.

Finally, the store opened, and there was a small party. Among the guests was Patrick's girlfriend, Margo. Theresa was devastated. She had been sure that she and Patrick had a future beyond the business. When she went home that night, she couldn't stop crying.

Two weeks later, Patrick called one night after Jennie was already asleep and asked if he could come over to her house. Without asking any questions, Theresa said yes. When he arrived he said that he had something to tell her. He wanted her to know that he and Margo had broken up. He said that Margo was jealous of Theresa, and they fought about it. Theresa didn't ask any questions because she wasn't sure what that meant. Patrick talked at some length about how Margo wasn't fulfilling his needs, which Theresa took to mean that he thought that Theresa would be able to. Finally Patrick asked if Theresa could have dinner with him that weekend. Theresa said Saturday would be good because her daughter would be with Theresa's ex-husband.

Patrick walked through the door on Saturday night to pick Theresa up, and within ten minutes they were on the couch with their arms around each other. They never made it to dinner. They also never spoke about what was taking place. Later in the evening, they did talk about their personal lives. Patrick told Theresa all about his relationship history. Theresa told Patrick all about the breakup of her marriage. What they never discussed is what had been taking place between the two of them.

Theresa and Patrick quickly developed a pattern. They went out every Saturday night, and Patrick stayed at Theresa's house through Sunday. When Jennie arrived home from her father's on Sunday evening, Patrick would often suggest that the three of them order in a pizza or Chinese food for dinner. He and Jennie would watch television while Theresa set the table and worked in the kitchen. Then he would leave before Jennie went to bed. For that one evening a week, it felt like a family.

At work, however, although Patrick did nothing to conceal the fact that he and Theresa were having a relationship, he also never did anything that made it appear that she was anything but an employee. He treated her no differently than he did everyone else; there was never one word or affectionate gesture that acknowledged the time they spent alone. In fact, Patrick rarely allowed their eyes to meet, and the bond that Theresa felt before they became a couple seemed remarkably less intense.

On their dates Theresa and Patrick went to movies; they went dancing; they went out to dinner with friends; and they talked about everything—except about what was taking place between the two of them. After several months, Theresa became disturbed by the absence of either verbal affection or commitment. One night, she said, "I love you" to Patrick. He replied, "I know you do." That bothered Theresa even more. But again, she didn't say anything. Theresa now admits that she was afraid to ask any questions because she was always concerned that she wouldn't get the answers she wanted. As much as she believed that Patrick really loved her even if he didn't say so, she also felt that she couldn't take anything for granted.

Then the holiday season arrived. Patrick came to her house the week before Christmas carrying a gift-wrapped box for Theresa, and an even bigger gift-wrapped box for her daughter. Theresa was surprised. She had been waiting for Patrick to say something about the holidays. In fact, she had been trying to find the courage to invite him over to spend either Christmas or Christmas Eve with her and her family. She was dreaming about a romantic holiday spent as a couple. Instead, Patrick handed her the gifts, saying that he wanted her to have the presents early because he and a male friend were going down to the Islands for Christmas.

Theresa was so devastated that she could barely speak. She couldn't even ask him if this meant anything for the future of their relationship. When he returned from his vacation, she noticed almost immediately that things were different. Instead of asking her out for Saturday, he made plans with her for Friday, but they went to a party and spent almost no time alone. The following weekend, Patrick asked to see her only on Sunday during the day, but Jennie was home, so they were never alone. At work, everything was the same, but at work, it had always just been business as usual.

Finally, Theresa summoned up her courage, walked into Patrick's office, closed the door behind her, and said, "What's going on?"

He said, "Nothing. . . . Why?"

Even though she was trembling, Theresa kept asking questions. "You're not dealing with me. What's going on between us?"

He replied, "I don't really want to talk about this here."

She said, "Well I think I do."

He said, "Come on Theresa, don't create drama when it's not necessary. I think we need to spend some time apart. I just need to sort some things out."

So Theresa asked the big question, "Don't you have any feelings for me?"

Patrick said, "Of course I do. I just don't know if I have the feelings you want me to have."

Later in the day, when nobody else was around, Patrick stopped by Theresa's desk. "Look," he said, "It's not you. It's me. I just don't see myself getting married or anything for a long, long time."

That was two weeks ago. At work, Patrick is friendly, cheerful, and casual. Although Theresa keeps up a good front, she goes home every night and cries. She can't figure out how anyone could be *so* casual. In the meantime, she's heard through the grapevine that Patrick is dating a woman who lives in the nearest big city. She is steeling herself for the time when this woman calls the office, and she answers the phone.

When I talked to Theresa I asked her if she was surprised by anything about Patrick's behavior. She said, "Not really surprised, just disappointed." She said that she always worried that Patrick wasn't really ready to make a commitment. I asked her if she had ever made it clear to Patrick that she wanted a commitment. She said no. When I asked why, she said because she was afraid that Patrick might leave her if she pushed in any way. I asked her if she had ever asked Patrick any questions about what he wanted from their relationship. She said no. When I asked why, she answered loud and clear, "Because I was afraid of what I would find out."

What Can We Learn From Theresa and Patrick's Relationship?

Taking a superficial glance at Theresa and Patrick's story, all we see is a relationship that didn't quite pan out the way Theresa hoped. Otherwise it seems like a relatively average boy-meets-girl situation. A closer look reveals that although the couple had a genuine friendship, the personal relationship between them never became fully real. At every stage, Theresa and Patrick could talk about everything *except* what was happening between the two of them. Neither of them articulated either their hopes or their intentions, for different reasons, perhaps, but with the same result.

What Could Theresa Have Done Differently?

Let's make a list of all the reality-based things Theresa might have done differently.

- When she heard about Patrick's reputation, she could have paid attention. Sure, a certain amount of gossip can always be discounted, but even so, since it was her heart that was involved, wouldn't it have been wise for Theresa to be sure that she was not personally vulnerable to Patrick until she had more information? She could have made a very large mental note that said: *Don't let your fantasies get out of control.*
- When they started having lunch together, Theresa could have easily asked questions in order to find out more about what Patrick wanted in the relationship department. She could have asked him if he had a commitment to anyone. She could have asked what commitment meant to him. Instead of being afraid to hear real answers, Theresa could have paid attention to make sure that she had real information.
- Theresa could have been very clear to herself about whether or not Patrick fit into the picture of what she wanted for her life. Was he really going to be able to change direction and turn into the family man she wanted? Or did he look like somebody who, unlike her, enjoyed being single and playing the field?

- She could have been very honest with herself—as well as with Patrick—about what she wanted from a relationship. She knew she wanted marriage and more children. She never said anything like that to Patrick because she was worried about scaring him off. This concern should have told her something.
- When Patrick asked her to work for him, she could have drawn in her breath and had the courage to start an appropriate conversation. She could have said, "What does this mean? Sometimes I think that you are attracted to me. Am I right about this? Sometimes I think I'm attracted to you. This may create some kind of stress down the line unless we are both honest about it. Let's discuss it."
- When Patrick came to tell her that he had split up with his ex-girl-friend, why couldn't Theresa have kept her defense system a little bit more in place. Why couldn't she have said, "What does this mean for the two of us?" Why couldn't she have said, "Let's not rush into any-thing until we talk about what we both want from each other," or "Let's put our hormones on hold until we make sure insofar as this relationship is concerned that we are both on the same page."

For Theresa there were always three separate and distinct relation-ships: The friendship based on shared interests; the personal relationship in which nothing was ever discussed or made real; and the fantasy relationship that existed in her own head.

Theresa was a victim of her fantasy life. There, Patrick was everything she wanted. In real life, he wasn't giving her what she needed. Instead of living in the relationship, she was living in hope. The minute she found someone who had a few of the important qualities she wanted from a mate, she pretended that everything else was a match. She drifted away from the real world, holding onto her fantasies as though they were a bal-loon. From the first moment, reality would have brought this balloon back to earth, but Theresa didn't want to be the one to burst the bubble.

What Could Patrick Have Done Differently?

Let's start out by acknowledging that Patrick wasn't motivated to do anything differently because he was never challenged. Theresa accepted everything. She was so happy about his good qualities that she never called him on the bad.

But let's say that Patrick wanted to be 100 percent responsible and caring—even if he knew that he was never planning to settle down with Theresa. What could he have done differently? How could he have behaved with more integrity?

- Patrick, like Theresa, could have been more accountable to reality. He could have looked at Theresa and her needs as a single mother realistically and behaved accordingly.
- Patrick could have made the initial "friendship" more honest by being more forthcoming about his personal life. In all probability he withheld the facts because he feared that if he was totally upfront about his psychosexual misadventures, Theresa might have been turned off.
- Patrick could have realized that you can't move from one woman to another the way he did without feeling confused and uncertain about what he was doing or feeling.
- Patrick could have played "truth" with himself as well as Theresa. He could have made a much more sincere effort to understand his own history and his tendency to move from woman to woman.

In short, both partners were having the relationship they wanted, but they were having it with themselves; it had very little to do with the other person. Theresa behaved as though this was a great love, and all problems therefore would be transcended. Patrick acted like a single guy who was dating and didn't know what he wanted. He had neither the courage nor the inclination to settle down for the long haul.

Neither Theresa nor Patrick was realistic about each other's real temperament or needs. They both told themselves stories.

AVOIDING THE FAKE SOUL-MATE TRAP

More than 150 years ago, a British poet named Elizabeth Barrett Browning wrote a poem to her beloved, Robert Browning. In it, she said "How do I love thee, let me count the ways..." Elizabeth Barrett and Robert Browning were considered by many to be soul mates, two poets who risked everything to run off to Italy to live together despite Elizabeth's failing health and the great objections of her tyrannical father.

We all love the idea of soul mates sharing a profound and powerfully passionate love. In fact, many of us spend our lives looking for the perfect soul mate. This causes difficulties in the relationship department because many of us typically deal with the soul-mate issue in one of two equally extreme ways.

- We are so anxious to find a soul mate that we almost immediately imbue potential partners with all the attributes of our soul-mate fantasies—even when these partners fall far short of our dreams. Those of us who do this need to open our eyes and be more realistic in the way we view our partners and our relationships.
- We are so determinedly perfectionist in our soul-mate fantasies that we reject loving, caring partners because they are a little bit less than perfect; consequently our relationships can never mature. Those of us who do this also need a strong dose of reality: We need to be more realistic about whether or not perfection is ever an option in this imperfect world.

For both these groups, and for all the rest of us too, a realistic attitude will go a long way to help us avoid all the fake "soul mates" who take up our time and keep us from finding the deep and true love we desire.

HAVING THE COURAGE TO LOVE = HAVING THE COURAGE TO MAKE A CONNECTION THAT IS BASED ON REALITY

People often think that having the courage to love means closing their eyes and having faith. It doesn't. We help neither ourselves nor our partners by failing to make our relationships real. In fact reality is the only way our relationships stand a chance.

I'd like to suggest that we each set up a system of reality checks for ourselves that we can use at different stages in our relationships.

A Reality Check for a New Relationship

When two people first meet, they create a foundation, a protocol, for how they will be dealing with each other for the life of the relationship. If we want our relationships to be loving and honest, we must start out by being loving and honest. Here are some things to ask yourself:

Am I telling the truth? Am I being true to myself and my needs and hopes?

It's essential that we start out by relating in a realistic fashion. Sometimes we are so anxious to impress our new partners that we say and do things that don't wash. Perhaps we subscribe to old-fashioned seduction techniques and aggressively promise the moon in order to get to first base. Perhaps we want so much to be liked that we fail to articulate our needs and passively go along with agendas that we really don't agree with. Help yourself by letting your partner know who you are and what you like. You don't have to say, "I'm an irresponsible sleaze who has never made a commitment to anyone, let alone myself." You can say, "I don't think I'm ready for any kind of serious relationship, and I plan to date for a few more years before I commit to any one person."

You don't have to say, "I'm determined to get married, and if I don't get what I want from you, I'm going to end up miserable and you're going to feel very guilty." You can say, "Marriage and family are very important to me, and I hope that I will soon meet somebody who will help me fulfill these goals."

In new relationships, we are sometimes afraid to reveal too much about who we really are because we are concerned that this information will scare the other person away. I agree that too much detail can be overwhelming, but I think an expression of basic intentions, attitude, and outlook is helpful. If you have serious intentions, and you scare away those who are casual, this would happen eventually anyway. Maybe it's better sooner than later so you can be free to find someone who wants what you want.

Am I asking questions that will tell me what I need to know?

You don't have to show up for a first date with a vial of sodium pentothal and a list of 3,000 intimate questions. But you could find out certain things. When you meet someone, for example, you need to know and pay attention to whether this person is married, engaged, or in another relationship. It seems silly to have to repeat this, but I still hear from so many people who were hurt because they failed to get this vital piece of information—or take it seriously even if they did get it. You also need to make sure that this person is "safe" and reasonable with a history of human attachments that can be verified. Again, I've received too much mail from intelligent sounding folks who tell me about having done fool-hardy things with strangers in the name of love. So find out what you need to know before you put your personal safety in anyone else's hands.

At the very, very beginning of a relationship, you want to establish for yourself that this new potential partner is capable of being present and real. You want to know what this relationship is going to be about. You need to figure out how emotionally and spiritually evolved this new person is. You want to be certain that he or she is truthful and honest.

Before you pledge your heart, have sex, or do anything to cement the relationship, you might also want information about the things that are really important to you: If you are an ardent feminist, you may want to find out what the other person's attitudes are about shared domestic chores and responsibilities. If you are a confirmed male chauvinist, you may need to know whether this woman is going to cheerfully and uncomplainingly wait on you. We stand a better chance of getting what we want if we ask the right questions before we make any leaps of faith.

Are we really talking?

You are establishing patterns that will probably be with you for the length of the relationship. As you begin to reveal pieces of yourself, notice whether or not your partner is genuinely interested in hearing what you have to say. Does this person make it easy for you to express yourself? Are you interested in hearing what he or she is saying? Is there a fair exchange, or is one person telling all the stories?

There are no rules for what two people can and will talk about. But it helps enormously if there is some basis for connection. You don't have to agree on everything, but it will certainly help the connection if you are able to respect and accept each other's point of view. It will help if you are able to share your opinions, ideas, thoughts, and feelings. It is essential that you can both "hear" and respond to what the other person is saying. This is real, and it's important.

Am I clear about the difference between following my heart and following my hormones?

Who hasn't been advised to "follow your heart." This even has a new age spin. Translation: if you can't follow your heart, you are stuck in an unevolved place. But let's be straight here: More often than not, when we think we are following our hearts, we are not. Sometimes we are following misguided fantasies; sometimes we are pushed by our fear; and still other times we are consumed by a hormonal flood that is totally compelling. The intensity of our yearning may feel as though it is coming straight from the heart, but it is not that simple or that pure.

The truth is that at the beginning of a new relationship, a full and powerful heart connection isn't there yet. It's much too soon. The heart connection is very complex and it takes time for it to fully form. Fantasies, fears, and hormones aren't at all subtle. They cloud reality and override wisdom, judgment, and *tender* feelings from the heart. You may be confused and think that it's your heart; you may even say it's your feelings. But you know that it can't be.

A short time ago I spoke to a woman who told me about going to a party and meeting a man who drove her home. They spent an hour necking in his car in her driveway. She wanted to know if I thought he would call her as he had promised. "What else can you tell me about him?" I asked. "Age, marital status, occupation, likes, dislikes." She said she didn't have any of this basic vital information. Why not? She gave me three answers: She didn't want to appear overeager, she didn't want to ruin the moment, and she didn't want to ask him anything that he hadn't asked her. This is a very sensitive woman. Nonetheless, she was so thrilled to find someone she was attracted to that she ended up necking with him before she felt comfortable enough to ask where he lived.

I cannot even begin to talk about the number of men who over the years have described being intensely attracted to a woman and then arriving at her place to discover that everything about it puts them on edge. He loves classical music, she has heavy metal posters. His idea of serious reading is the sports page, she has an apartment filled with bookcases. He isn't sure if he ever wants children, her three adopted children are asleep in the next room. Yet, the rush is so intense that the man continues forward, and before you can say "disastrous breakup," the couple is involved in the mismatch from hell.

Let's all admit it. There are at least two major forces that send us in directions that we later regret, and they often combine: (1) we genuinely want love and we hope the sexual connection will help us find it, and (2) we feel the intense urgency that is created by chemicals flowing through our little brains, our groins, and everything in between.

It's one thing to be a prisoner of your need to be loved and your hormones when you are seventeen, or twenty-two, or maybe even twenty-seven. But to be a victim in perpetuity and to victimize others in perpetuity is another story.

Fighting your desires is not easy. And it's not really something I feel comfortable recommending. But if your sexual desire has led you into self-destructive relationships, you have to ask yourself when you are going recognize reality for what it is. There is a big difference between a relationship that is meant to be and a relationship that is meant to be short and sweet. We know, going in, don't we, what possibilities a relationship really suggests. We often have a sense of what we can expect in terms of time frames, but urgency obliterates our ability to respect and act in accordance with that sense. Our urgency makes us act urgent. It makes us ardent, glassy-eyed, intense, and powerful, and completely confusing to others as well as ourselves.

If you have a history of relationships that haven't worked out, it might help if you slowed down and started making different decisions. Your decisions are not beyond your control. Remind yourself that hormones are just chemicals. Their compelling nature is not a constant; they simply provide an opportunity to lose your head in the moment. Remind yourself that sex and falling in love don't necessarily go together. Don't spin out of control and follow your fantasies with no respect or regard for reality. Am I sounding like a preacher here? Am I sounding like a schoolteacher? I haven't acted like one, that's for sure.

But about two years before I met my wife, I decided that I was not going to let hormones, fantasies, or emotional neediness control the show. For me it was a terrific decision because when I met her I wasn't off in another place involved in a troubled relationship.

Are we both allowing a genuine heart connection to develop?

A real heart connection is based on acceptance, trust, mutual respect, and love. When you barely know someone, you can only open your heart a little at a time. This is self-protective and realistic. Many of us are so very eager and anxious to develop a trusting heart connection that it makes us super vulnerable in the wrong way. My friend Joan, for example, admits that she is a pushover for men who spill their hearts and their guts on the first date. What she is only now beginning to realize is that many of these men are not genuinely connecting to her. They are just talking and venting, and they do it with everyone. My friend, Greg, has the same problem with openly neurotic women. Every time he gets into a relationship with one of these women, it is with the hope that, because of their problems, they will be able to understand his. It has never worked out that way.

When we develop real heart connections, we do it slowly and with great care. I trust you; you trust me. I accept you; you accept me. I will love your wacky sister because I love you; I will accept your out-of-control dog and spoiled cat because I love you. Slowly we build connections that last and that we can count on.

Are you realistically dealing with issues of safe sex?

Are you prepared to discuss safe sex, sexually transmitted diseases, birth control, and AIDS testing? These are realistic issues facing every couple who intend to have sex. Are you in agreement? Can you talk? Or are you sweeping the underlying issues under the rug while you fumble around for condoms? This is not a good sign. Sometimes the only way to approach it realistically is to say, "I have a very hard time talking about these things, but this is how I feel..."

Finding responsible ways to deal with issues of personal safety, health, and sex is a fine way for two people to discover whether they can combine reality with romance.

A Reality Check for a Relationship That Is Beginning to Be Serious

You have been out together more than a few times; you have probably opened the sexual floodgates; you have shared your war stories. You have heard about each other's problems, families, friends. How can you keep your relationship connected and honest? What questions can you ask yourself now?

Are my partner and I both on the same page?

Often, once a sexual relationship is established, we begin to be aware of the other person's intentions as well as our own. We begin to notice all the ways that our partner is not perfect. We all tend to do this *as soon as the relationship feels secure.* You do it, and your partner does it. This is okay. In order to be self-protective, you need to stay connected not only to your feelings, but also to your partner's. How serious are your reservations? How serious are your partner's?

Are either you or your partner trying to put more distance in the relationship? Are you both moving together at essentially the same speed? Have either of you erected insurmountable boundaries? In what ways are each of you withholding from the other? Does any of this deserve a real discussion? Notice what your partner is doing. Do you both have the same vision for the relationship you share or are your points of view so disparate that there's no chance? Now is the time to find this stuff out.

Are you being realistic about wanting too much or too little at this stage of the relationship?

Sometimes we sabotage a relationship's chances by pressuring for too much too soon. If you've only known each other for a few months, for example, it may well be unrealistic to insist on moving in together. If you can't trust the relationship, you can't trust the relationship. Cohabiting or even marriage isn't going to change basic problems. It may push them underground for a short while, but it is more likely that it will make them bubble to the surface and explode.

On the other hand, if you are both self-supporting adults who have been involved or living together for more than a year or two, it's unrealistic to believe that you can indefinitely postpone some form of formal commitment without making your partner anxious and insecure.

We keep our relationships real and honest by letting them develop at realistic speeds.

Are you responding appropriately to extremely negative behavior?

It's not going to go away you know. If he or she is regularly nasty or contemptuous, it will probably stay this way. If he or she acts out sexually with other people, this situation is not going to resolve itself without help.

If you did your homework when you first met, you should be able to avoid some of the more extreme examples of negative behavior. But the possibility of surprises always exists. If something really destructive is taking place, now is the time to open your eyes and let reality in. If this is going to be too much to live with long term, this is your chance to process this information and get out of the relationship *now*.

Are you fantasizing a future that isn't likely to happen?

Is your partner giving you a million and one signals that he or she isn't thinking long term? You can't avoid this kind of reality without hurting yourself. Sometimes having the courage to love means having the courage to face the fact that love is not a possibility in a specific relationship. If you want love, not heartbreak, you will have to move on.

Are you imagining that all the problems in the relationship will go away once you are married?

Victor thinks that once they are married, Betsy will become so enamored of married life her workaholic ways will disappear, and she will have more time for the relationship. Tammy is certain that once they are married and have children, Nathan will realize how much he wanted this all along.

Every so often I meet men and women who are utterly convinced that marriage will somehow magically do the work of therapy. Be real. As the divorce statistics prove, marriage doesn't cure anything.

A Reality Check for an Ongoing Relationship

You're both committed. You take each other so much for granted that it's scary. You are more concerned about the recently dented fender or the spot on the dining room rug than you are about the future of your relationship. What could possibly go wrong? What do you need to think about now?

Are you resolving problems as they occur?

One of the most dishonest things we can do in a relationship is allow our basic grievances and problems to fester unattended. Ultimately we strengthen connections by dealing with the stuff that bothers us as it happens.

When differences start to emerge it's a sign that the relationship is becoming more real. His/her driving, his/her preferred room temperature, his/her noisy friend Jack, his/her inadequate allotted closet space, and, of course, the old reliable issues du jour: hair in the sink and the squeezed tube of toothpaste. Don't hide these real disagreements under the carpet. These are real issues for the two of you to work out together.

This is a time to learn how to talk to each other gently about the real issues as they present themselves. This is a time to learn how to problem solve together. This is reality. Can you cheerfully settle disagreements? Can you learn to compromise? Can you survive not getting your way?

Are you able to keep your disagreements on a human scale?

Every couple has disagreements. Sometimes they hash these disagreements out. Sometimes they compromise; sometimes they are forced to agree to disagree. I know that years ago if I was going out with a woman I cared about, I was incapable of sleeping if we had an argument. I couldn't relax because I felt sick to my stomach and certain that the whole relationship would fall apart. I also admit that I waged every fight as though it was the end of the world.

For me, on some level, every fight, even if it was about the television clicker raised at least a small question of "Is it over?" One of the things I found most attractive about my wife was her ability to fight in the context of "I'm not going anywhere; we're just having a disagreement."

Learning how to keep conflicts scaled down to a reasonable and realistic level is one of the first things we all need to do to keep our relationship grounded in reality. That means giving up all the high-drama behavior and language associated with unstable relationships. That means no slamming doors; no throwing of heavy objects; no ultimatums or threats; no "either" we do it my way, "or" I'm leaving; and absolutely no revenge tactics.

Are you listening to each other?

Earlier this morning, I went for a little walk, and I happened upon a garage sale that some neighbors were having. The couple involved was having a bit of a low-key argument. The issue was that the husband had just sold a perfectly good vacuum cleaner for ten dollars. The wife, who was indoors at the time, had planned to ask for fifty dollars. He was saying: "Okay, I'll give you forty dollars. Forget it." She was saying: "It's not the money. If you didn't know the price, why didn't you ask? I was ten feet away. Why can't you ever communicate?" She seemed really frustrated. He seemed really annoyed.

Often we stop listening to each other.

Are you doing the necessary work to keep the love connection alive and vital?

It's very easy to build a relationship around shared goals, children, or even shared possessions and material values. The goals can take over, the children take over, the house and its contents take over our lives.

Then one day you look up, and the connection is no longer there. You're not listening to each other; you're not talking to each to her. It takes real effort to keep bringing your thoughts, energy, and love back to your partner. It can sometimes seem so much easier to simply turn on the television, get on the phone, or open the book you're reading and retreat into your own aloneness.

Here's a final reality that you always need to keep in mind: Just because you're married to each other doesn't mean you are connected. The bond will not maintain itself without real work. Ties keep coming undone. The connection needs constant reworking. So summon real energy and find real time to spend together to talk from the heart, or do something you both enjoy.

Romance and Reality Can Exist Simultaneously

My goal here is not to take a giant hose and squelch every romantic thought or feeling you could ever have with a blast of cold water. What a drag that would be. I like to think there's a lot of romance in my life. Why shouldn't it also be in yours? But I have learned that romance can be the *result* of the strength of the connection. It can be borne out of something real, and this is what I wish for you.

It's fine to be romantic—wonderful to be romantic—as long as you can also be pragmatic. One doesn't preclude the other, unless you choose that to be the case. Love, by its very nature, is romantic. And the stronger the bond, the more romantic it can be. I'm not trying to stamp out romance. I'm just trying to keep you from getting lost in the woods.

> It's fine to be romantic, as long as you can also be pragmatic

The point is that there needs to be an overriding intelligence to the way you conduct your romantic life, whether you are in hot pursuit or being hotly pursued. You need to be balancing your fantasies and intense feelings with clear thoughts and self-protective choices. If you can't create a balance—if you are feeling powerless in all of this—this is not a healthy sign that you are fully and completely in love. It is not a reflection of having found "great love." It is not a cause for celebration. If you are feeling powerless, it is a sign that you have either *chosen* to give up your power, or that you have been rendered powerless by an all-consuming need. Neither one of these are healthy or self-protective. And both deserve examination.

If your heart is open, there will always be room for romance. But you cannot trust that the universe will protect you just because you are in love. The universe will only protect you if you are protecting you.

CHALLENGE FIVE

The Courage to Allow
Yourself to Be Known

I am often approached by people who tell me that they are in distress because they are unable to get a sense of resolution after the breakup of a relationship. A common statement that these people make: "What really upsets me is that I feel as though he/she really never knew who I was." Often these men and women believe that if they were somehow able to go back and make themselves known, the relationship would have had a different outcome. Although they usually don't realize it, what these people are all saying is that even though the relationships that they are mourning may have had passion and excitement as well as great potential, the partners never truly connected.

There can be a world of difference between dating someone exclusively and actually making a connection with that someone. There can be a world of difference between having sex with someone and making a connection; there can be a world of difference between living with someone and making a connection; there can be a world of difference between being married to someone and making a connection—even if that marriage has lasted thirty years. And, though I know this is something you don't want to hear, there can be a world of difference between loving someone and making a real connection.

Over the past fifteen years I have interviewed hundreds and hundreds of couples—dating couples, married couples, living-together couples, sleeping-together couples—and I have personally known many more. And if there is one thing I have walked away feeling over and over and over again, it is the painful emptiness that comes from spending time with two people who say they are "together," but are, in many more ways, still strangers to each other. No matter how many years they have shared, each partner has kept huge chunks of himself or herself secret and apart.

In some ways the secret to intimacy boils down to five simple words: allowing yourself to be known. Without this crucial relationship ingredient, the prospects for real and lasting commitment are, at best, tenuous. I have seen this in countless relationships, and I have felt it in many of my own.

Ask Yourself: Is This Intimacy or Is It Ritual?

When a relationship is in its infancy, courtship is a series of rituals. Lions do it, moose do it, big-horn sheep do it, and we humans do it too. We have rituals for phoning, rituals for dating, rituals for seduction, rituals for sex. "Don't say this, don't ask that." "Wait two weeks," "wait six months." Our conversations are ritualized, our dress is ritualized, our day-to-day interactions are ritualized. And hopefully, somewhere amid all of this structured interaction, we have a few moments to truly be ourselves.

But being ourselves is not a high priority when the game of love is afoot. What most of us hope for is that later, when the relationship solidifies, we will have that chance to be ourselves. Those of us who are less optimistic may not even have that hope. And those of us who are truly terrified don't even *want* that chance.

What I have found, over so many years of writing and interviewing, is that for the majority of couples, "later" never comes. What starts as ritualized mating behavior becomes a permanent model for intimate interaction. And I hesitate to use the word intimate. We date, we live together, some of us even get married and have children, but we never struggle to make complex, genuine connections. We interact with our partners through stereotypes and learned behaviors, instead of struggling to be ourselves. The guys do "the guy thing." The women do "the woman thing." And we stay on the "safer" road.

Whether it has been six days or years, the patterns remain intact. We greet our partners every night with a kiss and we talk about the weather. We talk about the news. We talk about the neighbors. We talk about our children. We talk about our work. We talk about our pets. We talk about our politics. But we don't talk about ourselves, and we discourage our partners from talking about *them*selves. Our moods, our anxieties, our fears, our suspicions, our insecurities, our anger, our happiness, our sadness, our feelings in the moment, our feelings about each other . . . it never feels like quite the "right time" to bring these up. We may talk—some of us never stop talking—but we don't talk in a way that leads to deep connection. And when we feel the need to be intimate, we satisfy that need through sex.

Ask Yourself: Are You Building a Couple or a Caricature?

Over time, and it doesn't take that much time, we become caricatures as people. He becomes "the problem solver," she becomes "the nurturer"; he becomes "the guy who doesn't talk about his feelings," she becomes "the one who's always perky"; he becomes "the one who works too hard," she becomes "the one who works even harder." She cooks, he cleans. She shops for food, he takes out the garbage. She putters, he tinkers. He watches television, she surfs the web. Everybody keeps very busy, safely protected by our roles. And when we want to feel closer, we have sex.

Not surprisingly, the relationship itself can also become a caricature. We become "the couple that always travels" or "the couple that never goes out" or "the couple that never argues" or "the couple that always fights" or "the couple that never has sex" or "the couple that's always having sex." Instead of challenging these caricatures, we accept them and support them with our behavior because it seems far easier to play simple roles than to make a genuine connection.

Where Is the Commitment?

Now here's the six million dollar question: What happens to real intimacy and real committed connection in the midst of all of these stereotypes and "safe" behaviors? And here's the six million dollar answer: They have no place to flourish.

So we're together for six weeks or six months or six years or sixty years, but instead of growing closer, we grow apart. We're never really *together*. Instead of forging a more and more powerful bond, things skip across the surface. We share our time, but we don't share our selves. And while we may feel like we are part of a couple, we also feel very separate; sometimes painfully separate. And this is why it is so easy for so many relationships to suddenly fall apart. Because simply being together is not enough to keep a relationship from falling apart. Being monogamous is not enough to keep a relationship from falling apart. Being married, as the statistics show us, is not enough to keep a relationship from falling apart. And even though it may feel very bonding, having regular sex is not enough to hold a relationship together when two people are, in so many other ways, not connected at all.

Having a connection, and keeping that connection vital, demands that both partners are endlessly struggling to make themselves be known. Being "known" is the glue that keeps people connected and committed to each other. It is the thing that turns strangers into true and lasting partners. Being "known" not just in the biblical sense, but in *every* sense. It makes you care. It makes you love. And it allows you to be cared for and loved.

Here are some questions to ask yourself about your relationship patterns and whether or not you make yourself known to your partner:

- Do I play roles in my relationships that limit my self-expression? How do these roles make me resentful?
- Do I play roles in my relationships that keep me feeling distant? How might these roles keep my partners at a distance?
- Do I play roles in my relationships that keep me from feeling valued as an individual? Do these roles make me feel invisible or replaceable?

What Does It Take to Let Yourself Be Known? Going From Rituals to Meaning . . .

Some people don't want to be known. These people are so terrified of being trapped in a committed partnership that they do one of two things: They either remain completely inaccessible as human beings or they choose completely inaccessible partners—Like Frank who never answers his phone. Or Brenda who is always on an airplane. Or Christopher who only goes on dates when he is away from his home town. Or Simon who only dates women who barely speak English, which is the only language he knows.

And some people struggle to make sure that their partners never reveal who they are. Like Arthur who keeps up such a stream of steady chatter that his dates never get a chance to open their mouths. Or Ruth who looks bored every time her partner tries to discuss something that really interests him. Or Brian who becomes tense and leaves the room anytime he can't control the conversation.

All of these people practically walk around with signs around their necks that say, "Don't try to get too close." They say they're not looking for a long-term relationship. They say they're not looking for commitment. *It is your job to pay attention to their "sign," and take this message very seriously.*

But more of us at least *begin* our relationships with the hope of actually having a real connection. Yet we continue to fail. I am convinced that one of the primary reasons we fall short of our goal over and over again is because we fail to let our partners know who we are, and we also fail to give our partners the chance to be known.

Allowing yourself to be known means abandoning failed defense systems and unproductive game playing. It means dismantling inappropriate boundaries; it means becoming vulnerable; it means allowing your human qualities to shine through. Many of us have gone through our entire lives never letting ourselves be known to anything more than a personal diary, or to one very best friend. Why? Because there may be nothing more scary in the entire world than showing up for a relationship with nothing to offer but yourself.

we fail to let our partners know who we are

It's one thing to go with your partner to the movies, or out to dinner, or dancing till dawn. But it is another thing entirely to let your partner into your world: to let him or her know who you are from the time you get up in the morning till the time you fall asleep at night. It means exposing your likes, dislikes, moods, opinions, fears, hopes, and habits. More than anything it means allowing your partner to know what you think and feel; it means showing your partner who you are as a person, and who you are in the world.

I'm not talking about giant, cosmic, "if I ruled the world . . ." stuff. I'm talking about real world stuff. The things you feel every day, the things you see every day, the things you worry about every day, and the things you wonder about everyday. And nothing is insignificant. Nothing is too small.

It could be something as simple as the letter you just received that made you cry. The magazine article that made you laugh. The argument you had at work. The emotional conversation you had with your sister. The problem you had at the post office. The problem you're having right now. Do you keep these moments to yourself, and keep the feelings to yourself? Do you constantly censor what you will or will not share? Do you avoid sharing your reactions "in the moment"? Are you afraid to speak your mind? Are you a "collector" who waits till you have an avalanche of unprocessed material inside of you and then suddenly explodes? Do you keep yourself in a separate world?

Every time you stop yourself from making these little "bridges" to your partner, you lose an opportunity to strengthen your bond. Letting your partner into your world, and keeping him or her inside your world, that is the essence of letting yourself be known. And it is the path to lasting connection. Not holding back. Not being politically correct. These individual moments in your life *are* your life. These details and nuances of your life are your life. The range of feelings you go through every day—both with your partner and out in the world— are your life. Keep it all hidden behind fearful boundaries, and you are keeping your life hidden.

This is not supposed to happen on your very first date. And it's not supposed to happen all at once. It can't, and this should not be your goal. This happens in small pieces, over the course of time, with each piece getting its chance to be digested and processed. When a relationship begins, it may feel like the hardest work is behind you. But it is actually still in front of you in the form of a lifetime of bridge-building. If you stop, at any time, the development of the relationship also stops. And all too quickly the connection becomes brittle and fragile.

For most of my life, I had a secret inner dialogue running as a subtext throughout my relationships. To my partners, I was the well-intentioned, understanding, easy-going partner who rarely made waves. But inside my head, waves were crashing everywhere. Inside my head I was a very different partner; a partner who got angry or scared or hurt or depressed or critical or confused. But I rarely let anyone know. When I had a rough day I kept it to myself. When I disagreed or didn't care, I feigned the opposite. I dismissed the details of my life as unimportant, even though they were important to me. At the time I felt that I was doing the right thing by keeping much of my life to myself. I thought I was doing the right thing by keeping my feelings to myself. I thought I was doing the right thing by keeping my *self* to myself. But what I was really doing was drowning my relationships in the waves inside my head.

Do you do this too? How do you behave with your partner? Ask yourself these questions now:

- Am I able to share my life with my partner? Or do I dismiss talking about myself as being unimportant?
- Are there details of my day-to-day life that I always keep to myself?
- Do I consciously censor my feelings? Do I question my feelings before I express them? Do I often deny them or dismiss them entirely?
- Do I react "in the moment," or am I always waiting for a "better time," or a "safer way" to speak up?
- Do I have an "emotional vocabulary" that I can use without becoming angry or unduly upset? Can I utter simple sentences that express my feelings? For example: "That makes me upset, and I'd like to tell you why..." or "I'm happy when I'm with you because..."

A Love "Too Precious for Words"

"Don't speak...don't speak..." she pleaded, with a finger pressed to his lips. If you saw the film *Bullets Over Broadway*, you probably will never forget Diana Wiest's oscar-winning performance as the eccentric actress whose love for a young playwright was far too precious for words. She would not let him express his feelings. She would not let him express his fears. She would not let him express *anything*, so fearful was she of shattering the perfection of the connection she felt inside.

But as we saw in the film—and as we see in real life all of the time—our perfect connections are not always that perfect when fully exposed to the light of day. And a love too precious for words is usually a love too fragile to last.

Sometimes love may indeed feel too precious for words, but that feeling must eventually give way to some practical communication if we are going to survive the transition from fantasy to reality and build a comprehensive connection. Being known means breaking the precious silence regularly to speak not just from our hearts, but from our minds and our guts. And it means doing this regularly and continually throughout the lifetime of a relationship. If you can't break the silence, you need to question why. The answer is probably not "out of love," but "out of fear."

WHEN FEAR KEEPS US FROM BEING KNOWN

Karen has been seeing Emil for the past five months and she is convinced she has found her "soul mate." Karen can listen to Emil's stories for hours—just hearing him talk is enough to make her happy. Which is a very good thing, because Emil talks a lot. As he talks, Karen feels the bond. She agrees so strongly with everything he says. She relates so strongly to everything he feels. She is so envious of the life he has led. And so impressed by his accomplishments. Just being by his side and listening to him talk makes her feel that his accomplishments are her accomplishments, and that their future together will be the future she has always hoped for.

But here's the problem. Karen rarely talks. She never interrupts Emil during one of his stories, unless it's to offer him tea. She doesn't ask questions when she is confused. And she doesn't challenge Emil's perceptions or opinions even when she vehemently disagrees. Karen has formed such a powerful connection with the fantasy of Emil that she has lost her connection to the real Emil. Because he is the *kind* of man she has always dreamed of, she isn't ready to risk discovering if he is a someone she can actually have a relationship with. So her lip remains buttoned, keeping herself from being known. And she doesn't ask the hard questions that would help her truly know Emil.

How does Emil feel about this relationship? Does he feel connected to Karen? Does he feel as though he has met *his* soul mate? Or is this the way he is with *everybody?* And is Karen merely a good audience. Could Emil tolerate being challenged? Is he interested in hearing *Karen's* stories. The only way Karen can get the answers to these questions is by letting herself be known. Emil has had an interesting life, and Emil *may* be a wonderful person, but Karen won't know if Emil is capable of making an intimate connection until she starts letting herself be known. She has to challenge her own internal boundaries. And she has to challenge his boundaries too. She has to challenge her own fears. And she has to do this on a constant basis to get the relationship she deserves.

Tony met Kathryn at a New Year's party and they danced together till three in the morning. It was the kind of beginning you see only in the movies. Guy sees woman across a crowded room. Guy fights his way across the crowded room. Guy says hello. Woman smiles. And the next thing you know they're dancing.

On paper, Kathryn is Tony's dream. She's tall, long-legged, athletic, and self-assured, with a smile that melts hearts. She has a good job. She has a nice apartment. She has a solid education. And she loves having sex with Tony. But here are a few of the problems that Tony is already willing to sweep under the rug. Kathryn doesn't talk to her family, and she won't tell Tony why. Kathryn doesn't like Tony to sleep over after they have sex, and she won't tell Tony why. Kathryn has no close friends, and she won't tell Tony why. Kathryn says that her job comes before everything else, and she won't tell Tony why. Kathryn won't let Tony buy her *anything* and she won't tell Tony why. Kathryn won't take a vacation with Tony, and she won't tell Tony why. Kathryn won't spend time with Tony's friends or family, and she won't tell Tony why.

The fantasy Kathryn is quite appealing, but the reality Kathryn is an enigma. Yet Tony is so in love with the fantasy, that he is willing to live with the missing pieces. When Kathryn says "I don't want to talk about it" Tony doesn't press the issue. When Kathryn says, "These are my rules . . . ," Tony doesn't complain. When Kathryn says something that makes Tony angry, he keeps his anger to himself. Even when Kathryn completely contradicts herself, Tony doesn't make a point of it. Tony doesn't trust that he can let his feelings be known without creating a problem in the relationship. What Tony isn't quite ready to face is that he already has a problem. Kathryn has impossible boundaries that keep her from being known. Tony is terrified of those boundaries, and that keeps him from being known.

Too many of us lose sight of reality when our fantasy needs get engaged. On paper, at least, we have found the partner we want, and we are determined to make it work. So we ignore the things that make us uncomfortable, the things we question, the things we dislike. And we keep our doubts deeply buried inside where they can't rock our fantasy boat. What kind of relationship does this leave us with? A relationship of little substance. A relationship we have no real reason to trust. A relationship that has no foundation. And when the first big storm blows through our lives (a personal crisis, a big fight, etc.), relationships like this rarely survive.

Ask yourself the following questions:

- When you have problems with what's going on in your relationship, do you have the courage to express yourself and challenge the status quo?
- Do you accept less because you don't have the courage to ask for more?

Letting yourself be known means having the courage to express your feelings, doubts, conflicts, enthusiasms, and opinions. This is not about being controlling, inappropriately demanding, or petulant. It's not about screaming, and it's not about whining. Letting yourself be known means being able to calmly voice differences as well as being periodically willing to face honest and tough dialogues. It means not letting grievances pile up. It means being able to say, "I don't agree." And "I don't like that." And "That makes me uncomfortable." And "That hurt my feelings." And "I'm feeling very angry." It means not saying, "I'm fine," when you're really not fine. It means not saying, "nothing's wrong," when many things *are* wrong. And it means processing information and feelings as they come up, not warehousing feelings and letting your grievances pile up until you feel alienated and disconnected. All of this takes courage.

DO YOU KNOW THE DIFFERENCE BETWEEN BEING NAKED AND BEING KNOWN?

It begins with a phone call, a date, or a friendly hello. Then we start to dance. We flirt. We fantasize. We question. We yearn. We take long walks. We have long talks. We survive the ups and downs, the nervousness and awkwardness, and regular bouts of uncertainty. But then SEX enters into the picture, and everything magically shifts.

Many people feel that a relationship truly "begins" when sexual intimacy begins. And for many years I was one of those people. As long as the two of you are fully clothed, you're nothing more than "friends." But the moment the clothes come off, you instantly become a couple. Sex, seen as a symbol of acceptance, signals the end of the initial courtship phase and the start of "something special." Tensions melt. Fears dissolve. And everyone starts to relax. But what too many people "relax" into is a pattern of not connecting.

One of the biggest shortcuts on the road to *dis*connection is the shortcut spelled s-e-x. I'm not saying this because I'm prudish and I'm not saying this to discourage people from having sex. I'm saying this because it is something I see constantly in my work (and because it is a trap I have fallen into many times). The development of a sexual relationship may indeed be a signal of relationship beginnings, but far too often for too many couples, it's when the "relating" *stops*. Instead of being a celebration of connection, sex becomes the principal way we connect. And for some, the *only* way we connect. But is this connection enough?

Sex has the potential to be one of the most intimate things two people can share—an extraordinary physical bond that can flood us with feelings of emotional connectedness. And this is truly wonderful. Yet for many people, sex is a substitute for real intimacy, or even a way to *avoid* intimacy. And that often leads to disconnection. Take Nick for example.

Nick's idea of "being really intimate" revolves around seduction and sex. As far as he's concerned, when undergarments drop to the floor, the relationship has started. And as long as they keep dropping, everything is going just fine.

When Nick is feeling distant from his partner, sex is his solution. When Nick is feeling angry or jealous, sex is his solution. When Nick needs assurance or wants to express his caring, sex is his solution. This is the way he has always been in relationships.

Nick truly feels he is sensitive and loving. He feels he shares his feelings. He feels he is interested in his partner's needs. But he is doing it all through sex. He thinks that should be enough. But his partners don't always agree. Nick has been "stunned" at least half a dozen times in his life by women who have broken up with him for what he calls "no apparent reason." "One moment we're sleeping together, having incredible sex," he explains, "and the next moment she's telling me she wants to see other people. I've never understood it. And I've never understood the reasons."

Yet Nick *should* understand because he has also handed over his fair share of unpleasant surprises. Many times in his life he has lost interest in a woman he was sleeping with and brought the relationship to a sudden end. How does he explain it? He says, "it just wasn't working." But my explanation is a little different. Because when I look at Nick's relationships I see that while he did have a connection with these women, the connection was little more than a sexual one. And it was not enough.

There is more to connection than physical intimacy. Much, much, much, much, much more. Physical intimacy is fabulous and important, but in the absence of emotional intimacy it is simply not enough. Not if you want a committed relationship. Sex alone does not stop people from being strangers—sometimes it insures they will remain strangers. Sex alone does not create a rich bond. Sex alone is no guarantee of commitment. Sex is not superglue. And it takes courage to keep sex in its place.

DO YOU ACCEPT SEX AS A SUBSTITUTE FOR INTIMACY, EVEN THOUGH YOU KNOW THE DIFFERENCE?

Vanessa has been living with her boyfriend Abe for almost an entire year, and she wishes she could be celebrating. But Vanessa is beginning to fear that the relationship with Abe will never go anywhere but to the bedroom. Vanessa wants a partner. Vanessa wants commitment. Vanessa wants real intimacy. But in her relationship with Abe, all she gets is good sex.

In the beginning, Vanessa was thrilled. The sex was so exciting and highly charged that it made her feel close to Abe very quickly. Yet she has to admit, if only to herself, that the connection has never deepened. The few times that Vanessa tried to talk about her feelings or her needs in the beginning of the relationship, Abe immediately shut down. Since then she has shied away from ever rocking the boat. And she has learned to accept sex as her only consistent opportunity to meaningfully connect with Abe; it is the one arena where she doesn't experience emotional boundaries.

There is more to connection than physical intimacy.

It's not that Vanessa doesn't trust Abe. She feels he really does care about her as much as he can care about anybody. And she is certain that he isn't "going anywhere." The problem is that as far as she is concerned, the relationship isn't "going anywhere" either. She can't talk to Abe about the relationship. She can't talk to Abe about her life. She can't talk to Abe about her feelings. He has all of these boundaries she can not cross, and she feels that she is "starving." Abe is using sex to avoid a deeper connection, and Vanessa is feeling the brunt of that.

Vanessa doesn't want the relationship to end. In many ways she feels lucky to have found Abe. But she doesn't know how long she will be able to survive in a relationship that lacks more intimacy. She has turned to her friends to feel more fulfilled. She has turned to her work to feel more fulfilled. She has turned to the television to feel more fulfilled. But the emptiness doesn't go away.

Vanessa is an interesting example because Vanessa *knows* what she is missing. Many people feel thrilled to have a sexual connection they can count on. That is their definition of "being known," and they have no hope for something more. But Vanessa knows that "something more" is the richness of a more comprehensive connection. And she knows what it means to "be known." She just can't take the steps to get there because she fears it would cost her this relationship.

But if "being known" costs you the relationship, what kind of relationship do you have? And what is it exactly you will be losing? Sexual intimacy is terrific, but it doesn't pay the emotional bills—it doesn't feed you like a real connection, and it isn't a connection you can trust to last. There is a huge difference between opening your arms to welcome a physical embrace, and opening your heart to let someone in. If you know the difference, you cannot accept less with the hope that it will some day feel like more.

Ask yourself the following questions:

- Do I sometimes allow sexual connection to become confused with emotional intimacy?
- Are sex and physical affection my first solution to relationship struggles?
- Do either I or my partner ever seem to use sex as a way of avoiding emotional intimacy?

If you answered yes to any of the above questions, you need to begin to learn to express your feelings and thoughts outside of the bedroom. It's up to you to perfect non-sexual ways of expressing intimacy and resolving arguments.

When You Talk, Do You Also Listen?

Dinah loves to talk. And talk and talk and talk. Dinah would tell you she is a great communicator. But no one who knows Dinah would agree. Because Dinah doesn't really communicate, all she really does is talk.

Dinah doesn't monitor her own conversation, to get a sense of how and where her words are landing. She doesn't leave room for the other person. She doesn't look up to see if she's connecting. She asks almost no questions. And she doesn't really listen to what anyone else is saying. Yes, she has some great stories, and yes, she can fill a room with sound, but she doesn't know how to make connections that go beyond the superficial.

When Dinah is alone, with no one to phone, she feels empty. She hasn't let herself be known to others, and she hasn't given others a chance to be known to her, and the lost connections are experienced as emptiness. This confuses her, particularly because she feels she has so many friends. But it's actually very easy to understand. Her talking creates boundaries to intimacy, fending off the possibility of a bond she can feel.

Dinah thinks that having a partner could fill this emptiness. But the reality is that only learning how to be known, and how to give others a chance to be known, will fill the void she feels. Her eyes and ears need to be open. Her heart needs to be open. It's not enough to simply talk.

Do You Resist Asking Tough Questions Because You Don't Want to Be ASKED Tough Questions?

There are times when every relationship isn't working out perfectly. That's when we most need to talk instead of close down. When problems occur in your relationship are you able to ask the tough questions that might help bring you closer together or tell you what you need to know? Ask yourself:

- Do I sometimes change the subject or tune out my partner's answers when I'm not hearing what I want to hear?
- Am I afraid of being asked tough questions that would reveal my fear of getting too close?

- Am I afraid of being asked tough questions that would reveal my vulnerability?

Your relationship with your family is troubled, so you don't ask him about *his* family. You hate talking about your job, so you don't ask her about *her* job. You're embarrassed by your relationship history, so you don't ask him about *his* history. You struggle with financial woes, so you don't ask *her* about her financial integrity. You question your ability to stay in a committed relationship, so you don't ask him how *he* feels about commitment.

Many of us, afraid of being asked the "tough questions" that relationships prompt, avoid asking these same questions to our potential partners. We think we are being self-protective. We think we are being egalitarian. We think we are being clever and avoiding our own discomfort. But what we are really doing is setting ourselves up for disappointment, alienation, misunderstanding, confusion, unattainable fantasies, and perhaps even a great deal of trouble.

Building a relationship requires asking hard questions, and surviving a lot of questioning. It requires revealing a lot of unpleasant information. It requires building a complete picture—a picture of yourself, and a picture of your potential partner. Not on the first phone call or first date, and not all at once. But it is something that must ultimately happen. And though it calls for a lot of courage, the sooner you begin, the smarter you are.

Is Creating Crisis Your Way of Avoiding Being Known?

Many people who are terrified of being known still haven't faced their own truth. They say they want a *real* connection, they say they want a committed partnership, and they are always going through the motions. Yet there is a part of them that seems dedicated to making sure this never happens—a part that makes sure they are never known.

There are many ways to fight off the possibility of intimate connection while going through the motions of being in a relationship. And one of the most effective ways is by always creating a crisis. Consider Ellie, for example.

When Jeff met Ellie she was studying to get certified as an emergency medical technician, and she told him she couldn't handle any additional stress. When conflicts arose between them, Jeff felt he had to remain silent, afraid that Ellie couldn't handle it. Two weeks after Ellie took her exam, a former co-worker had to be hospitalized for almost a week. Ellie visited the hospital every single day, always coming home exhausted. Jeff continued to stockpile all of the conflicts he experienced in the relationship because he was afraid Ellie couldn't handle any more stress.

Soon the holidays arrived and Ellie was dizzy with commitments and always trying to play catch-up. She had invited fifteen people to her apartment for Thanksgiving and she was in a complete panic, having no idea how she would accommodate them. She spent almost two weeks preparing while Jeff continued to put important relationship issues on hold. December arrived and Ellie was hopelessly behind in her Christmas shopping and would spend her evenings at the mall. Jeff silently stewed at home, waiting for the mall to close. After Christmas Ellie asked Jeff if they could go away somewhere to celebrate the New Year. After scurrying to make last-minute plans, the couple took off for Florida. On the plane when their long weekend was over, Jeff finally got up the courage to voice some of his concerns. Ellie got so angry she refused to speak. And the relationship ended that day.

Life is difficult. And challenges do arise on a regular basis. Friends get sick. Jobs can be in jeopardy. Cars get hit in the parking lot. And the stock market crashes. But if living in your house is like living at the fire department, you need to examine your contribution to the endless calamity.

Granted, there is a certain kind of bonding that happens in a crisis, but it is not the kind of bonding that lays the groundwork for a solid future (and if you think you are using crisis to create and intensify your bonds, you are also heading down the wrong road). Solid futures are created in "peacetime," not wartime, when you are relaxed enough and centered enough to process a complex variety of relationship issues that vary from the incredibly obvious to the deceptively subtle. There is a certain kind of deep connecting that only happens when things are calm, not when you're putting out fires or racing across town. If a solid future with a partner is what you crave, you have to be willing to stand still and open intimate doors. And if you are avoiding opening those doors—using ongoing crisis as a way to put up boundaries—you must begin to ask yourself why. And yes, I know, this takes courage.

- Do my relationships seem to go from crisis to crisis? Why?
- Do I ever use crisis, even if it has to be manufactured, as a way of avoiding deep connection? Why?
- Do I have a tendency to immerse myself in the drama of my partner's life, abandoning my own priorities and needs? Why?

Do You Have Obvious Boundaries That Keep You From Being Known?

It is a painful paradox, but so many people who say they are searching for a more connected relationship also continue to cling to boundaries that thwart the very possibility. I was one of these people with many obvious boundaries for many years of my life. Are you one of these people still? If you use phrases like, "*my* work," "*my* friends," "*my* family," "*my* house," "*my* drawer" on a regular basis, you probably are. You don't have to actually say it; if that's what you are thinking, you are creating a huge sense of separateness. And you are denying both yourself and your partner the chance to be known.

For some people, these walls are very intentional. They don't want anyone to get too close; they don't want to let themselves be known. And this is their way of insuring that the relationship can not progress past a certain point. But many more people create these boundaries out of role-playing, out of habit, out of archaic behaviors that stem from family styles and sibling rivalries, and out of shame. If you are one of these people, there is a great deal you can do to change the future course of your relationships.

This is not to say that you must merge every single aspect of your life with the life of your partner. And it is not to say that you are not entitled to keep many things separate. But it is so important to become more aware of the "my's" in your life, and to understand that each time you use the word "my" you are pushing a potential partner just a little bit further away. The goal in relationship is to bring your partner more and more into your world, piece by tiny piece.

So stop right now and take a good look around you . . .

Take a good look at the *people* in your world. Your family, your friends, your co-workers, your many acquaintances. How many of these people do you let your potential partners know well, or even know about at all?

Take a good look at the *places* in your world. Your office, your recreation spots, your favorite bar, your weekend escape. How many of these places do you let your potential partners know well, or even know about at all?

Take a good look at the *things* in your world. Your house, your car, your furniture, your appliances. How many of these *things* are you able to share with your potential partners?

As we're going to get to commitment, we have to find more ways that we can become fully connected to our partners. Allowing them access to our world is one of those ways. Clearly, these connections must happen in stages. You don't want to open every door of your life on day one. But look at the doors that you never open, and the doors you discourage potential partners from opening, and consider how they keep you from being known, and keep your relationship from moving forward. It takes real courage to look at these doors, and even more courage to start opening them. But this is how we make the transition from being alone, to being in a partnership we value.

How Many Secrets Do You Keep to Yourself?

Who is the you nobody else knows? Do you have a family history you would never share with a partner? Do you have a personal history you would never share? Is your life pretty much an "open book," or do you live a life full of secrets you could never imagine sharing with even the people you love most? Think long and hard before you give an answer.

Do you have emotional problems you've never talked about— such as depression, anxiety, obsessions, compulsions, phobias, or rage? Do you have substance abuse problems you've never talked about? Sexual abuse problems you've never talked about? Financial problems you've never talked about? Food addictions? Shopping addictions? Gambling addictions? Jealousy problems? Sibling rivalries? How many significant areas of shame are there in your life that you've never talked about? Contrary to the popular literature, there *is* such a thing as "big stuff." And this is all big stuff.

I'm not saying that you should rush right out and let the whole world in on your secrets. I'm not even suggesting that you should be telling your partner. Some of this material needs to be handled with the wisdom and support of a caring therapist or counselor before it can go *anywhere* else. And some of it never *should* go anywhere else. But you need to understand how each of these secrets keeps you very separate. They keep you from being known, they build walls that can not be penetrated, and they seriously affect your capacity to connect.

And what about the "smaller stuff"—things you may not consider significant. Do you have a secret stash of chocolate, a porno collection, a romance novel you're always reading? Do you eat ice cream on the sly, occasionally drink a little too much wine, or sneak out of work and go to the movies on days you're feeling bored? Once again, I'm not suggesting that your life should be an open book, with no secrets kept for yourself. Yet you need to understand that little secrets quickly add up to become a concrete obstacle to connection. Not necessarily an overwhelming obstacle, but a significant one.

Maybe you're not ready to share the "big stuff" today, and maybe you never will be, but sharing the "small stuff" is also very powerful. Sharing the small stuff helps your partner understand who you are by giving him/her a richer, more interesting, more complete picture of you. You may find this hard to believe right now, but the quirks that you're trying so desperately to hide are also the quirks that make you special or endearing. Your obsession with lip liner. Your concern about your receding hairline. Your nickname in second grade. Your cereal box collection. The funky way you clear your throat. These are the things that make you unique. These are the things that make you fascinating. These are the things that make you wonderful, that give you depth and breadth. These are the things that a partner can love, and want to keep on loving. It takes real courage to be this human with another human being; it is the kind of courage that leads to a lasting bond.

WHY DO YOU KEEP *YOU* HIDDEN?

If these secrets are so much a part of who you are, why do you keep them hidden? The answer to this question is a five-letter word, and that awful word is: shame.

Shame is the killer of connection. Shame is the killer of relationship. Shame drives us all into isolation and loneliness. Shame is the enemy of commitment. But shame is also something each and every one of us struggles with every day.

If you are like most of the men and women I know, at some point in your history you learned that it wasn't always safe to open yourself up to the people who are closest to you. Perhaps you were ridiculed by classmates or siblings. Perhaps you were scolded by parents or teachers. Perhaps you were misunderstood. Perhaps you were ignored. Perhaps you were rejected. Perhaps you were even completely abandoned. Whatever it was that happened to you, you learned to close off parts of yourself. Your world was not always an accepting, understanding, supportive place. It was not always a loving place, certainly not unconditionally loving. It could also be a very dangerous place. A painful place. It is where you learned to "play it safe." And it is where you learned about shame.

But lessons like this are not easily forgotten. And many of us closed off those "parts" for keeps. We have constructed boundaries that we do not question, and we will not negotiate. If these boundaries are threatened, we panic. And if they are threatened too much, we run. This is our way of playing it safe, our way of insuring we are never harmed again.

Playing It Safe Isn't Playing for Keeps

If you knew that your secrets kept you separate, if you knew that they silently sabotaged your ability to make a lasting, loving connection, would you still labor to keep them hidden? Or would you labor to make them known?

We think we are playing it safe when we hold back parts of ourselves from being known. But for every part we hold back, the integrity of our connection suffers. Hold back too much, and the connection slips away.

In relationship, as in most aspects of life, there is really no such thing as playing it safe. Wearing masks is fun on Halloween, but it's a ghoulish way to live your entire life. Withholding important information isolates us from the ones we love most. Withholding crucial feelings makes us prisoners of separateness. In the absence of "big pieces" of who we really are, we struggle to feel connected, and our partners struggle too.

It is very painful to be rejected. And I wish I could offer you a magic formula to insure that this will never again happen to you. But, in my opinion, it is a far more painful thing to be rejected without ever being known. Or to go through the motions of relationship without ever being known. Or to live in a marriage without ever being known. It is a far more painful thing to lose your chance to find commitment and connection, because you didn't have the courage to be who you are. Yes, it takes real courage to let yourself be known, and to never stop letting yourself be known, but the rewards more than justify the risk.

Don't Be a Stranger Anymore

Many times in the early stages of my relationship with my wife I can remember looking at her and thinking, "I don't really know this person at all." And I am certain that she often had the same feeling. Even after being together for several years, there were moments when this strange sensation would surface. Yet both of us have been very committed to breaking down internal walls and revealing, for better or worse, who we truly are and how we truly feel. Because of this commitment I already feel, after only five years of being together (and two years of marriage), closer and more connected to my wife than I do to anyone else in my life, including people who have been close friends for dozens of years. This closeness is not a product of living under the same roof or sleeping in the same bed. It is a product of endless attempts to be known and understood. The feelings of love and loyalty that emerge from this powerful connection hold our relationship together in the face of the serious frustrations, difficult challenges, and (yes, we do have them) hard-fought disagreements. Being known to each other has allied us more powerfully than any oath or piece of paper ever could.

When two friends part, one will often playfully say, "don't be a stranger..." This is the advice I wish to give you now, but I am not being playful. If you want a real connection, one that is gratifying and has the ability to last, you can't be a stranger to yourself, and you can't be a stranger to your partner. The more you know yourself, let yourself be known, and encourage your partner to let him/herself be known, the more capable you will be of forming the kind of bond you desire. Yes, this is very difficult, and yes, there is a lot of risk, but there is far more risk when you choose to keep your essential self hidden. A commitment to a relationship requires something more than hard work. It also requires faith—faith that taking risks will bring you closer to each other—and, of course, a steady stream of courage.

CHALLENGE SIX

The Courage to Learn
The Lessons of Acceptance

*G*wen and Leonard are both seventy-something. When you see them walking down the street arm in arm, the caring connection they share seems obvious as well as enviable. Eavesdrop on their conversation, and you'll hear all the stories and feelings that the two of them continue to share. Married for close to forty years, they are still very much in love. Gwen says that as far as she's concerned, acceptance has been the major lesson of the marriage.

Gwen and Leonard agree that over the years, they have both stopped trying to change each other. They have come to fully realize that no two people are ever perfectly matched, and that there will always be some disagreements. Gwen says that the couple came to an understanding years ago: Whenever either of them felt truly annoyed by something the other partner did or didn't do, instead of criticizing or provoking an argument, he or she would first stop and think about how important the relationship was and try to be more accepting of the other's foibles.

Intimacy and acceptance are directly connected to each other. Yet, men and women with commitment issues are almost inevitably confused about the role acceptance plays in finding and keeping love. Your ability to accept a romantic partner with all his/her human imperfections is a true measure of your capacity to love. After all, don't most of us want to be accepted for who and what we are? Yet how many of us are mature and caring enough to be lovingly and appropriately accepting of our mates?

Unable to Be Intimate / Unable to Accept

Amy has never been able to accept any man as he is, nor has she ever been able to accept any relationship she has been part of. What does she say about the men she's known? Different things. Not smart enough. Not engaging enough. Not experienced enough. Not sophisticated enough. Sometimes she sounds like the all-knowing Oz.

Amy's friends shake their heads in bewilderment at her behavior: although she finds fault with every man she's known, she doesn't necessarily find fault with the right things. Her friends are completely blown over by her capacity to tolerate huge problems while she instead focuses on silly stuff. It doesn't seem to bother her, for example, that her current boyfriend is a totally self-absorbed jerk who never stops talking about himself and his tedious career. No, what Amy can't accept about Dan is that he went to what she calls a substandard college. Amy's last boyfriend Larry was a genuinely kind and intelligent man, but Amy couldn't accept him because he was, according to her, too "small town" and "had the shoes to prove it."

I can identify with Amy because I remember having some of the same feelings and history. I would say that I wanted to meet women who were complicated and "interesting," then after meeting such women I would reject them because they had "too much history," which is of course what made them complex and interesting. And I usually didn't have to search for these "somethings" to reject. They appeared quickly and automatically, and it all seemed perfectly reasonable to me. I didn't feel as if I was fishing for excuses. These things were plain as day. Several women *were* "older." Several others *were* "younger." One *hadn't* been exposed to big city cultural activities.

Looking at Acceptance and Image Issues

I also identify with Chuck, who can easily be described as the quintessential commitmentphobic man. He has commitment issues in all areas of his life, which is not unusual for someone with this kind of fear. Chuck has a difficult time committing himself to a decision about which car to buy let alone which woman to spend his life with. To him, each car, no matter how wonderful, projects another kind of image, and he's not sure if that's how he wants to be seen. Safety is important to him, but he would never buy a Volvo for example because it might be viewed as a family-type car, and he's a single-type guy. On the other hand, he would never buy a sporty two seater because he doesn't want to appear as though he is too slick and terminally single.

Like many men and women, Chuck looks to externals—clothes, cars, friends, watches, neighborhood, and women—to project a very clear and firm message about himself to the outside world. Every woman he's known has been a casualty of his image issues. When a woman looks, talks, acts a certain way, he falls in love. But usually as the relationship progresses, and the woman becomes more human, a switch flips in his head, and he becomes acutely aware of her shortcomings.

I understand Chuck because it took me years of work to undo many of my image issues. I was, for example, always captivated by "knockout" women as well as European women, who I viewed as being sophisticated by definition. When a woman looked the part, it was amazing—even to me—how much crucial information I could overlook. I accepted all the wrong things. What I couldn't accept were simple human foibles. There were wonderful women with whom everything felt perfectly fine when we were alone together. But when we were out in the world, I found myself distancing myself from them because they didn't quite measure up to my off-the-wall notion of the image I wanted to project. Small insignificant human imperfections often became tragic flaws that I couldn't accept. I certainly didn't believe that my attitude compromised my capacity for intimacy or commitment. But of course it did.

When two people first meet and fall in love, it can sometimes appear as though they are of one mind. On the first date, for example, the average guy is happy to go to what he might call a "chick film" just to be with "her" and hold her hand. But when he comes back into his body and remembers that he really prefers a different kind of movie, he becomes less willing to accommodate someone else's preferences. Typically when you first meet someone you like, you don't care if this special someone buys skim milk, whole milk, or goat's milk. But as the relationship progresses, these things begin to matter. For men and women with serious commitment issues, these things can begin to matter way out of proportion to what is taking place.

As men and women with commitment issues become more secure with their partners, they typically begin to feel uncomfortable and closed in. Unable to accurately pinpoint the source of their discomfort, they blame the relationship. The classic reasoning is "If only I could get out and get away from this person, I would feel better...I would feel free." Typically these men and women then begin to find fault with one or more of what they believe to be their partners' intrinsic qualities. Usually these are qualities that existed at the beginning of the relationship, when they were accepted wholeheartedly.

For example, Hector, a forty-two-year-old writer, has been living with Susan for two happy years. Now, as they begin to talk about marriage, he is backing off. He hasn't told anyone but his best friend that he is concerned that Susan's breasts are too small.

Jean thought her boyfriend was perfect until they got engaged. Now she worries that he is not outgoing enough and doesn't make enough money.

Harry has got himself in a situation where he is torn between two women, each of whom is wonderful in different ways. Naomi is tall, thin, elegant, and blonde. Brandi is petite, adorable, funny, and brunette. What a choice! He can't decide which woman he would like to be with forever.

It all sounds so superficial, doesn't it? But if the truth be told, often we begin and end relationships for just such superficial reasons. It's easy to come up with a laundry list of reasons why we can't accept a specific person as a partner, and these reasons rarely have anything to do with the depth of the human connection.

What Is It That We Don't Accept?

The struggle to become more accepting seems like an external struggle. Doesn't it feel as though the focus is on something external? She has a problem with his hair. He has a problem with her makeup. He wishes she had a better sense of humor. She wishes he had a better job. Yet, for people with commitment issues the inability to accept the totality of another human being usually has its roots in an internal struggle, a struggle that begins with internal discontent.

Your problems with acceptance are often nothing more than a projection of the contempt you have for what you perceive to be your own shortcomings. You say he/she isn't successful or smart enough for you because somewhere inside you feel insecure about how you appear to the outside world. You criticize his/her fast track career because somewhere inside you are unhappy that you didn't push yourself harder, or worried that you can't compete in a fast track world. You criticize the lack of sophistication in his/her paintings because somewhere inside you are concerned that your friends will judge you harshly based on your mate's talent. You criticize the close relationship your partner has with his/her parents because you are unhappy with the lack of closeness in your own family.

What your criticism is really spelling out is that you want a partner who has the power to make you feel better about you. This means that you have taken all your problems and concerns about what people will think about you and dumped them into your partner's lap.

Trust me on this one: Much of your inability to accept your partner's human imperfections has its roots in a lack of self-acceptance. How do I know this? Because if you were more content inside of yourself, you wouldn't be so tough on everyone else. People who are more at peace with who they are, what they do, and what they have tend to be far more accepting of others. They are genuinely more easy going and open hearted. Someone else's blemishes don't bother them. Someone else's quirkiness doesn't bother them. Someone else's limited vocabulary doesn't bother them. Someone else's career choice doesn't bother them. It's just a blemish. It's just a quirk. It's just words. It's just a career. It's not a big deal. They don't think everything about their partners reflects on them.

People who accept themselves tend to be far more accepting of others

If you are going to get to a place of acceptance, you are going to have to start with a rigorous internal inventory of where dissatisfaction lurks inside of you. What are your areas of shame? Where are you vulnerable? Where do you pick yourself apart? Where do you feel "less than"? What are your greatest sources of internal dissatisfaction? Why do you need someone else to be a certain way for you? Why is it not enough that they are just who they are?

Understand, once again, that many of these internal struggles may not be fully conscious. Unconscious conflicts tend to make us far more critical, judgmental, and dissatisfied than those conflicts that are already on the surface. But look at those areas where you are withholding approval, and try to imagine where the roots may lie.

Try also to imagine that this same critical voice of yours was once a voice that others used against you.

What made you feel that your looks were not good enough, that your brain was not good enough, that your choices were not good enough, that your ... was not good enough? What made you feel that *you* were not good enough? And how have you turned that around today? The more you feel that you are good enough, the more you will be able to open your heart and find and accept appropriate partners. If you know you are wonderful, you will be able to accept and appreciate your choices.

GOING TO THE OTHER EXTREME: IS THERE SUCH A THING AS BEING TOO ACCEPTING?

While some men and women accept nothing, others almost pride themselves on their capacity to accept the unacceptable. Take Michelle for example. When she met Bob a year ago, he told her that he would walk on water for her. Within a couple of months, however, she found herself doing all the work in the relationship. She was always the one who had to run out to get the tickets; she was always the one running to the store to buy food for Bob to eat; she was always the one adjusting her needs to accommodate his schedule, moods, and desires. She was even carrying the water—the gallons and gallons of bottled water that Bob drank while he was at her house because he couldn't accept the taste of her tap water.

Then Michele discovered that Bob was also dating and having sex with someone else—every Thursday night in fact. Bob told Michele that he loved her; however he felt he needed more time to break off this old relationship, which existed before he met Michele. Michele accepted this explanation. She even believed Bob when he told her he was no longer having sex with his steady Thursday night date.

For months Bob told Michele that he would be going on a one-week business trip to California, and he invited her to come with him, saying that he would have plenty of time for relaxation and sightseeing. Michele asked her boss for vacation time, bought clothes, arranged for someone to walk her dog. Two days before they were supposed to leave, Bob told Michele that there was a change of plans: his company altered its policy, saying that since this was a business trip, Bob couldn't combine business and pleasure. Michele was very disappointed, but she accepted the situation.

To show Bob what a good sport she was, Michele decided she would surprise him by seeing him off. When she got to the airport, she saw Bob preparing to get on the plane with another woman. Michele ran to the ladies' room so that she would not be spotted, but when Bob finally returned from California, she confronted him. Bob told her that he was very upset about having to lie to her, but he didn't know how to tell her the truth: that he felt that this other woman was too fragile to handle his abrupt departure. He saw this as a good-bye trip that would help the other woman get over the relationship. Michele is now trying very hard to accept Bob's version of what is taking place.

Michele isn't alone in her misguided interpretation of what it means to love. Women and men accept all kinds of rotten behavior in the name of love. They foolishly believe that if they are appropriately self-protective, their capacity for love and acceptance are somehow being compromised. They really think that all this inappropriate unconditional acceptance is going to win them some fabulous door prize. Remember the song "What I Did for Love"? Michele and others like her need to learn that a personal relationship is not the place to emulate Mother Teresa. And, of course, we all know that Michele isn't really accepting Bob for the dishonest manipulative creep that he is. What she is doing is accommodating his pathology in the hopes that the relationship and her love will create a miracle and *he will change.*

Of course it's unlikely to happen. And most important, Michele's misguided acceptance and accommodation is keeping her from finding a better partner.

What Michele and others like her need to understand is that often we find our way into abusive relationships because we don't fully accept ourselves. We think that something is so profoundly wrong with us that we are prepared to accept all kinds of negative behavior. "Who could really accept me," we think to ourselves. "I am so much less than perfect; I have so many problems; I have such a dysfunctional family; I'm such a failure; I have such a less than perfect body/mind/education/career/earning capacity."

Some people are so conscious of their self-perceived faults that they have literally articulated the "deal" in their heads. "I will accept the fact that he refuses to make a living if he will accept my heavy thighs and messy closets." "I will accept her nagging if she accepts my workaholic habits." "I will accept his drinking if he accepts that I avoid sex." The problem of course is that often we are only making deals that the other person hasn't agreed to. Michele, for example, accepted Bob's infidelity, but then *he pushed the envelope.* As Michele struggles to maintain the relationship—hoping all the while that Bob will change—his behavior escalates, and he becomes even more outrageous.

A lesson that we all have to learn: **Acceptance does not mean tolerating a partner's rotten behavior in hopes that he/she will change.**

Here's a partial list of some things that we should not accept: partners who are physically, emotionally, financially, or verbally abusive; partners who are unkind to our children, our pets, our friends, or our families; partners who are unfaithful or untruthful; partners who fail to act with good intentions; partners who don't want the best for us; partners who undermine our achievements.

Moving to Connectedness—What to Accept

If you want to have a loving connection with another person, it helps if you are very clear about what acceptance means. Here are some suggestions for incorporating a more accepting attitude into your life.

Accept Love

Accepting love can be very difficult for those of us with commitment issues. That's because we are often confused about what love is and isn't. We confuse love with longing; we confuse love with passion; and we confuse love with heartache. People with commitment issues typically know what it is to pursue new partners; they know what it is to pine for a good relationship; they know what it is to try to please the person they care about. But often they don't know how to accept love. Love makes them uncomfortable.

People with commitment issues may spend their lives pursuing the possibility of long-term love with reluctant or unavailable partners. While they are doing this, they usually experience all-consuming feelings of longing and heartache. This lifestyle calls for great psychic energy and tolerance for pain. But it is easier for many of us to be in these terminally dissatisfying relationships than it is to accept love in our lives. We sabotage love and fight it off; we run away from it and denigrate it. We rarely realize what we are doing or why we are doing it. Even when we ourselves can be very caring, the bottom line is that those of us with commitment issues find it difficult to be with someone who cares about us in the same way. It's difficult to let someone love us. Truly love us. What's that about?

Some of us don't trust love. Some of us don't recognize love. Most of us don't believe love will last. It makes us feel guilty; it makes us feel vulnerable; or it makes us feel "weak." It makes us feel dependent; it makes us feel insecure; or it makes us feel out of control. These are all things we don't want to feel. So even if we can accept grand passion with all its intensity, we have the hardest time accepting basic, human, grounded, well-intentioned love—the kind of love that begins and flourishes in the absence of high drama and hormonal overflow. But this is the very thing, and perhaps the only thing, that enables a relationship to grow and last.

Accept Who You Truly Are and How You Lead Your Life

Adam, a teacher, is an average-looking man and a bit of a bookworm who is only attracted to actress and model types—the kind of women whom every man in the room is eyeing. In the meantime, half of the women at work find him incredibly attractive, but he never notices them.

Babette is a thirty-nine-year-old divorced mother with two daughters she adores and overwhelming expenses; the only men who seem able to get her attention are unemployed hunks in their twenties. She gives a cold shoulder to average looking, employed, nice guys.

Jacob is really involved with his religion and is trying to find a spiritual path. He is also interested in finding a life partner. So why is he looking for *her* in the local bar instead of investigating activities that might attract women who share his interests?

JoAnne says she wants a "family values" husband more than anything. With that in mind, she has tried to convince one high-living, hard-drinking, womanizing man after another that he should change.

Many of us struggle with an inability to accept who we truly are and what kinds of partners are best for us. Instead of being driven by our strengths, we are controlled by our limitations. We are not honest with ourselves, and we are not true to ourselves. We make a lot of bad choices. We do a lot of brainless stuff.

Yes, sometimes opposites do attract, and it can be interesting and exciting to cross over into a world that is not really yours. But these crossover dreams rarely provide a good framework for a relationship. In fact, they are often a way of avoiding relationship. Sooner or later you have to come back home to who you are and to what your life is. You can flirt with other worlds for a while, and you can try to be a "player," but you're not going to win in this league—even if you do manage to keep your head above water—if it isn't congruent with who you really are.

Accept That Your Partner, Your Relationship, and, Yes, Even *You* Will Never Be Perfect

People always ask me if they should *settle* for a less than perfect relationship. The word *settle* bothers me. So does the notion of less than perfect. If you are in a basically good and loving relationship, you are not settling. This is a gift that deserves time, effort, and care.

The only perfect partner is the one who got away, the one who doesn't want you, or the one who married to someone else. Partners are only perfect in our fantasies. If someone is sitting in a room with you long enough, trying to make a real connection, his or her less than perfectness will automatically appear. As will yours. You can go through life chasing the unavailables and convincing yourself that if these people were to love you, it would all be the stuff of fantasies.

Remember this: *no one person will ever fulfill all your needs.* It simply can't happen. A woman I know said that she once had a blind date with a man we'll call Gary. Gary was in his late forties, and he had never married. When my friend asked him why, he replied. "Well, I didn't marry my last girlfriend, Martha, because she couldn't cook like my previous girlfriend, Jacki. And I didn't marry Jacki because she couldn't ski like Paula. And I didn't marry Paula because she didn't like to go to parties, and she also didn't look so hot in a bikini . . ." Gary's list went on for close to thirty minutes.

All of these women could have been right for Gary, or none of these women could have been right for Gary. We'll never know. Neither will he. What it's pretty easy to figure out is that Gary never gave any one of these relationships his best shot. These women never had a chance. None of these relationships ever had a chance. And unless Gary's attitude changes, he doesn't have a chance.

Accept That Your Partner Is a Separate and Unique Individual

Don't you want your partner to be like you—to like the same food, enjoy the same movies, belong to the same political party, attend the same worship service, have the same personal habits, values, and priorities—all the time? Wouldn't that be great? Or would it be annoying and boring?

What we often hope for in a relationship is a complete merger. Two heads and hearts that beat as one. But, one of the lessons of long-term love is accepting the many ways you and your partner are different. You let bills, accounting records, and tax forms pile up until the last moment; he/she attends to them as they appear. For as long as you can remember you had this dream that once you fell in love, you and your partner would order in Chinese food every Sunday night and watch old movies; he/she hates Chinese food and doesn't like to see any movie more than once. You are so rigid about your toothpaste ritual that you even have a little gizmo that you replace faithfully on each new tube so that the toothpaste can be rolled up evenly as it is used; you love your gizmo so much that you gave your partner one just like it. Your partner reacted to your gift by laughing for a full fifteen minutes.

Accepting and incorporating another person into your life in a vital, meaningful way has nothing to do with a symbiotic merging that is both unhealthy and impractical. The two minds that think as one, two hearts that beat as one is an unworkable fantasy. Two people cannot be fused together. Nor should they be. In the best of situations, no matter how strong the initial attraction and bond, letting someone become part of your life is something that happens in tiny little increments.

No matter how much time you spend with another person, no matter how many interests you share, no matter how passionate your sexual connection, you are not becoming your partner. You are not taking over your partner's life, and your partner should not be taking over yours. As a loving relationship develops, ideally you are both becoming more visible for who you are as well as appreciative of the ways each of you is different.

two hearts that beat as one is an unworkable fantasy

My wife's stepfather, who is from the Midwest, is an avid bird-watcher who even writes a birdwatching newsletter. When I first met Jill she would go on and on about birds. Clearly, her stepfather had shared his passion with her when she was a child, and it had great meaning. Now I was born in New York City, and the only birds I had ever noticed when I was growing up were nasty pigeons messing up the windowsills. So when Jill first started pointing out birds in the trees, I scoffed in my best jaded-New-Yorker-who-has-no-time-for-nature way. This hurt Jill's feelings a lot, which made me stop and think about my rigid ideas. Today we have a large, gorgeous bird-feeder in our backyard that I bought for Jill as a birthday present. And now I must confess that one of the first things I do each morning is look outside to see if we have any winged visitors. It gives me incredible pleasure, perhaps even more pleasure than it gives Jill because it's still such a novelty for me. The point of course is that as I let go of my rigid knee-jerk reactions, I discovered something new and different that has widened my outlook; this, in its small way, has brought the two of us closer together.

As you learn to love someone more and more, I think you will discover that if you want your relationship to successfully endure, you can do one of two things: You can get angry over each and every way your partner is not like you, or you can see this as an incredible source of richness, something that adds to your life in ways you can't even imagine until it's actually happening. This is the process of relationship; this is the process of connection.

Accept Responsibility

We don't often think about it, but here's one of the reasons why it takes so much courage to love: Responsibilities come hand in hand with love and commitment. If you want mature, adult love, you have to bite the bullet and act like an adult. For many people, however, this is *the* biggest struggle. Anyone who hasn't dealt with his or her childhood losses and ghosts can have a difficult time transitioning into adulthood—no matter how old he or she may happen to be.

Each of us feels at least some resistance to fully growing up, and we need to work through this resistance before we can sincerely take on the obligations of a committed relationship. There are often valid reasons for this resistance. For example: If you're still trying to capture the childhood you lost; if you had to become a "little adult" before your time; if your innocence was robbed by abuse or neglect; if you still have a child inside you that isn't easily soothed, you may not feel ready to be an adult. You may not feel ready to (heaven forbid) bring children into the world and give them the time, attention, energy, love, and, yes, money they need—particularly if you didn't get that much support yourself.

People who feel cheated of a youth can have a genuinely difficult time being faithful, sharing money, and saying good-bye to school-yard game playing. If this rings a familiar note, you may need to grieve the childhood you lost before you take on adult responsibility. This doesn't mean that you have to head for the park with your kite, frisbee, and baseball bat every day for the next fifteen years to give yourself the time you lost. And needing this time doesn't have to spell out a lifetime of relationship failure. Find a therapist or a support group and try to understand how your feelings have translated into commitment conflicts. If you want commitment, the time has come to work on these issues and make some hard choices.

Accept Your Partner As Is

When Maeve married Thomas, she had a hidden agenda. Although she was head over heels in love with her new husband, she thought that she would be able to get him to change the way he dresses. With this in mind, she mapped out what she thought was a subtle game plan: She would buy Thomas new shirts, ties, pants, suits as gifts—Christmas, anniversary, Valentine's Day. Within a couple of years, Maeve figured that Thomas would have a whole new wardrobe, and she would have a husband who looked the way she wanted him to look. What happened instead is that within six months, Thomas was screaming, "I'm not your f . . . ing Ken doll!"

What Maeve fails to realize is that Thomas sees his clothing as a reflection of his values. He wants to wear inexpensive suits. He likes his worn-out shirts and jeans. They make him happy. As he has often told her, he knows how to shop for clothing; he knows how to buy different clothes if he wants them. He knows the difference between an Armani suit and the suits he wears. He doesn't want to wear an Armani suit. That's not his style.

Before you decide to elevate Thomas to some kind of sainthood, you should know that he also entered marriage with a hidden agenda. He thought that under his influence Maeve would become more interested in current events and world news. With that in mind, he began to read the *New York Times* aloud to her in the evening. Each day he comes home for dinner with a little bunch of clippings from the *Wall Street Journal* that he leaves for her to read. Sometimes over dinner, he pointedly switches on some news show on CNN.

What Thomas hasn't taken into account is that Maeve has an extraordinarily difficult job with a demanding employer. At night, she doesn't want to feel as though she is taking a seminar. Unlike Tom she is unable to look at the world news objectively. She finds the nightly news stressful and anxiety provoking. She wants to put on some music, relax, and hang out. Maeve hates Thomas's course in Government 101. She feels as though her husband is either lecturing her or testing her on how well she paid attention to what happened in the world that day. She finds it downright annoying.

It seems difficult to believe that Thomas and Maeve can be doing so much damage to their relationship by trying to mold and change each other, but they are. As they chip away, all they are creating is resentment and anger. It's easy to see that what really concerns Maeve is that her friends will think less of Thomas because of his well-worn corduroys. Thomas, on the other hand, likes the idea of seeing himself with a well-read, politically savvy woman.

It can be such a challenge to just relax and let your partner be the person you fell in love with. By definition, time will change both of you in ways that you didn't imagine. Five years down the road, Maeve could be a work-at-home mom who has become positively addicted to CNN; Thomas could end up with a job that requires more perfectly tailored suits and shirts than even his spouse can currently imagine. That does not mean, of course, that Thomas and Maeve can't make changes on his or her own in order to please each other.

Accept That You Can't Control Your Partner's Behavior. Also Accept That You Can't Control Your Partner's Friends, Family, Religion—Or Belongings

I know many women who complain bitterly about what they call "a masculine tendency" to be controlling. It's no surprise that I also meet many men who loudly complain about what they call "a woman's tendency" to be controlling. Control—who has it, who wants it—creates major problems in relationships. And control, of course, is diametrically opposed to acceptance.

Let's say for example that your partner comes with you to a party and strikes up a conversation with someone who is important in your life—a best friend, an ex-love, a sibling. They get along so well that they agree to have lunch after the party. This is clearly not a sexual connection, so you're not jealous, but for reasons you don't understand, you're uncomfortable. What will they talk about? What will they say? How come you're not a part of this? As we move to connection, we learn that we can't steer and control a partner's relationships—new as well as old. If your partner and your sister decide to become best friends, you have to let go of proprietary feelings for either one of them and accept that new and different levels of friendship and connection are going to become part of your life.

On a similar note, it's brutally unfair to say, "I love my girlfriend/boyfriend, but I don't want to have anything to do with his/her mother/brother/child/best friend/dog/cat." Your partner has relationships that existed long before your connection came to be. Admire your partner for maintaining these connections, and give up any ideas about trying to sabotage them. These connections will all change naturally as your relationship with your partner deepens and becomes more primary. Some of your partner's friendships may even dissolve—as will some of yours. But your connection to your partner will be weakened if you try to control or dismantle each other's old friendships or family ties.

Accept That Compromises Have to Be Made

Sleeping habits. That's one of the hardest areas in which Jill and I have had to compromise. When we first met, we both went to bed after midnight, and Jill set an alarm every morning for 7:15. She had to go to a formal workplace each day, and she also requires less sleep than I do. I used to tell people that I became a writer so I would never again have to set an alarm clock for the rest of my life. If I don't sleep a full seven or eight hours, I'm a veritable zombie, and I have a hard time concentrating on my work. And the piercing tones of an alarm are enough to ruin my day.

We had to find a way to accommodate each other's needs. Even though I already had a brand-new, terrific bed, we had to buy a new, firmer bed so I would be less conscious of Jill's movement, as well as a gentler alarm clock that I could learn to tolerate. Jill learned to tip-toe out and get dressed in another room. This wasn't fun, but we did it because the long-term survival of the relationship depended on it. This may not sound like very big stuff. But it is the kind of stuff that often drives two fundamentally well matched people apart.

I think it's important to remember that a compromise doesn't mean that one partner always has to cave in. Thomas and Maeve, for example, could compromise in the following way. Thomas could agree to buy some clothing that he would wear for those times when he accompanies Maeve to business-related events; Maeve could agree that she and Thomas would discuss current events over dinner at least one night a week.

Every couple will have their own little list of areas in which to compromise. Once you are in a committed relationship, you and your partner are sharing a joint fate. You are not the captain of this ship called relationship. There is somebody else who has the same set of controls you do and the same level of decision-making authority. But that person has a completely different headset and different priorities. And sooner or later, these differences will surface; if you are going to live happily ever after (or even happily for a week), you will have to compromise.

Accept That Your Partner Has a Life Apart From You

I know a couple who have been married for almost forty years. They both feel that they have a failed relationship. Yet to this day, they are rarely apart for more than an hour. *She* insists that he drive her everywhere she goes; he insists that she help him shop for socks. *She* resents it when he wants to play tennis without her; he gets annoyed when she talks on the phone to friends. It goes without saying that they are both immaturely jealous when either one of them speaks to someone of the opposite sex. Everything they do, they do together—bickering all the way. Now, I recognize that some couples seem to be able to spend all their time together in the context of a loving relationship, but many more can't.

I personally find it uncomfortable to watch couples who appear to be joined at the hip. I think it's important for individuals to know that they are individuals. I think it's important that we accept that our partners have separate friends and interests. Being part of a couple shouldn't translate into a limited or partial life—for either partner. In the context of a trusting relationship, separateness is a good thing. It is, in fact, a vital thing.

Accept Your Partner Into Your Life

Appropriate boundaries are one of the characteristics of a good relationship; inappropriate boundaries are one of the symptoms of a commitmentphobic relationship. At the beginning of a relationship, typically men and women with serious commitment issues appear to have almost no boundaries. They accept new people into their lives readily, willingly, and fully. Their conversations are peppered with plans about things "we will do." Then as the relationship progresses they pull back, allowing their partners less and less access into their lives. The relationship becomes an exercise in giving less, which is exactly the opposite of what one expects from a loving connection.

We all have clear issues about sharing our space, our time, and our emotions. Finding the courage to love means that you will have to find the courage to let someone else have some access to your space, your friends, your family, your things, and your thoughts. This is a process that takes time and can sometimes only be handled a little bit at a time. But if you want love, you have to know when and how to take down the walls and let the other person in.

How to do this isn't hard to figure out. The key words are *slowly* and *incrementally*. If you barely know someone, you don't want to promise that you will be spending the rest of your life or even New Year's Eve together. If you've been going out steadily for six months or more, and it's December 28th, it's inappropriate to suddenly want to spend New Year's Eve apart.

Accept That Relationships Come With Certain Built-In Trade-Offs

It's simply not fair to want all the perks of relationship without accepting the maintenance costs. If your partner cooks a great dinner, it's only fair to share in the cleanup. If you want a fully stocked refrigerator and clean underwear, you have to be prepared to visit the market and the laundry. Relationship implies working together. You wash, I dry. You vacuum, I scrub. Not, you do everything, I watch TV.

Now, let's take this one step further. If you're having a sexual relationship with your partner, it's not fair to think that infidelity is appropriate. It always makes me crazy to hear someone say, "What my partner doesn't know won't hurt him/her." Infidelity doesn't have to be in the open to hurt. Its very existence carves up the foundation of a relationship. It's the single most disconnecting, destructive act, and it reflects a serious corruption of someone's understanding of love.

It's also important to remember that it's extraordinarily destructive as well as unfair to engage in behavior that can have a serious impact on your partner's life, health, and well-being—and withhold information about that behavior. This is made even more true given the fact of sexually transmitted diseases.

Accept the Relationship on Its Own Terms

Like most people, by the time I was old enough to make any serious attempts at relating, I was completely filled to the top of my brain with "ways I was supposed to be." Often I deeply resented many of these "shoulds" yet I also expected things to be a certain way. I had, for example, very specific ideas of what a couple should do on weekends. Too much Paul Reiser and Helen Hunt reading the *Sunday Times* in bed or taking day trips to the country on Sunday. It was the cultural definition of togetherness that really messed me up.

In some of my past relationships with women, we did all that weekend stuff. Jazz festivals with friends, events with families, structured holiday experiences. I thought that's what it meant to be a part of a couple, and I wouldn't have dreamed of being different. I thought once you were a couple, you did most things together. You spent weekends together; you went to the movies together; you went to events together. I wouldn't have dreamed of doing stuff on the weekend if that stuff was alone stuff. And surprise of surprises, I was unhappy much of the time because *I didn't want to be there.* I wanted to be home or doing something else. But I didn't know how to do that.

I didn't know how to be an individual while also being a good partner. For me, once I was with a woman, I thought every activity should become a couples' activity. Every decision. Every everything. I believed that once you became a "serious" couple, you didn't get to do things alone anymore. And this made me unhappy. This is not to say that I wanted to "hang out with the guys" in pickup bars, or take dozens of trips to faraway places alone. But I always felt as though being in a relationship meant giving up my individuality and separateness.

Then I met Jill, and the picture was somehow switched. Jill had to work every single Saturday and most Sundays in the gallery where she was employed. Here I was with a partner who wasn't available on weekends. And I got angry. I wanted to be the couple going for drives in the country, going to visit friends, going to antique fairs and craft shows. I wanted all of it, which is amazing considering the fact that I *hate* most of it.

Jill's schedule forced me to look at how I arrived at my ideas of the way a couple *should* look and what a couple *should* be doing. Instead of stewing and hanging on to the resentment and frustration that I believed was caused by Jill's schedule, I decided to take the high road. To my surprise, it wasn't very long before my weekend idealizations began to dissolve. Today, even though Jill no longer works on Saturday or Sunday, there is a flexibility in our relationship that leaves room for couples' weekend stuff as well as individual weekend stuff. There is also room for no stuff at all. If schedules change, we will work together to accommodate those changes. I understand now that this is possible.

Accept That Sex *Will* Change

Tim, who just turned thirty-two, got engaged about six months ago. Now on the eve of his wedding, he is suffering from a serious case of cold feet. He has convinced himself that something is seriously wrong with his relationship. When he and Stephanie met and fell in love, they spent whole weekends in bed. Then they moved in together, and although the sex was still great, there were fewer and fewer weekend marathons. Now, four years later, they are about to get married, and Tim says that he is thinking more about relaxing on the beach than he is thinking about how Stephanie looks in a bikini. Sex changed! Does this mean that the relationship is doomed?

The fact is that sex inevitably changes, and more often than not, it becomes less intense. This is not necessarily a "bad" sign. In fact it's often a good sign that means that the two people are not as much "on edge" with each other. When the relationship isn't on edge, sex typically does lose its intensity. This may be one of the reasons why people fight just to amp up the sex. Familiarity doesn't bring intense sex, it brings more loving sex. It should not bring contempt. Nor should it bring a justification for infidelity.

Accept That the "Healing Power" of Love Has Its Limitations

Many people searching for commitment are firmly convinced that their most pressing problems will be resolved once they find the magic of a loving relationship. They are convinced that "the right relationship" will miraculously make them feel complete and happy all the time, as well as unconditionally accepted. They imagine that once they are in a good relationship, they will never again feel lonely, depressed, misunderstood, or at loose ends. And they use these fantasies as a way of judging the "rightness" or "wrongness" of any Mr. or Ms. with whom they become seriously involved.

The problem here is that the unpleasant feelings we carry inside don't automatically disappear because we are in loving relationships.

Once the pink bubble of new love begins to disappear, we inevitably discover that we are not happy all the time; we are not content all the time; we are not buoyant all the time. There are times when we still feel lonely, angry, depressed, misunderstood, and even sometimes unloved. This has much more to do with the emotional issues you bring with you into a relationship. These issues stay with you because they stem from powerful internal struggles. A loving partner can make a difference, but a loving partner isn't going to heal all of your pre-existing difficulties. To judge this as a failure of the partner or the relationship is to judge harshly and incorrectly. In fact, sometimes the relationships that seem instantly to take away all of our pain are the relationships that deliver much more unhappiness down the road when the fantasy bubble bursts.

Accept the Human Condition

Birth, death, aging—these are all themes in long-term commitment. This is a lot of reality for *anyone* to deal with. One reality issue that has always disturbed me, for example—and I know it disturbs a lot of us— is the reality of aging. It's embarrassing to admit this because it seems so superficial. But it's the way I feel, and I think we all have things that we can only admit to ourselves. As nervous as I am about the idea of aging, for example, I was always even more nervous about being with a partner who is aging. How can you tell how someone will age? How can you know about someone's health down the road? Someone's mind? Someone's looks? Will your beloved get wrinkles or cellulite? How will you feel when the one you love can't remember where he or she parked the car? Or whether there even is a car? I often asked myself whether I would be able to accept another person's aging process.

I remember discussing this repeatedly with a wise therapist. I would ask her what I would do if things crumbled twenty years down the road. Was I so superficial that I would need to exit the relationship? Would I be one of those men who trades in a fifty for two twenty-fives? What this therapist was very quick to point out was that I was frightening myself by trying to leap into a future that I couldn't possibly visualize with any accuracy. At that point in my life I had no understanding from experience; I couldn't imagine the depth and strength of the kind of connection that comes from twenty-plus years of being together and possibly even raising children together.

When we make a commitment to one single partner, in many ways we are erasing the idea of limitless possibility, at least in the dating department. We are accepting the fact that we are now adult, and we are now part of the human continuum. We are no longer thinking about "who we will marry when we grow up." We are grown up, and we have *made* our choice. Wow. That's hard. That's a lot like saying that we are mortal, and that we are going to age, and that someday we too will die, just like everyone else. In fact, it's exactly like saying that. No wonder commitment can be so scary. Yet, one of the profound ways we enrich our lives during the time we have on this earth is by establishing long-term connections and commitments. Connection and commitment make life worth living.

Acceptance Leads to Compromise

Where will we eat? Where will we live? Where will we spend the holidays? Will we open the windows at night or keep them closed? Will we split every bill down the middle? How much time will we spend with our friends? How much time will we spend with each other?

Relationship is, ultimately, all about compromise. When you are with another human being you love, you will compromise on the largest issues, the smallest issues, and everything in between. Sometimes you will get lucky, and you and your partner will be in perfect, almost seamless, agreement. Much of the time, however, you will both have to struggle together toward a place in the center—which is where real relationship occurs. If your relationship is going to be balanced and solid, this process is unavoidable.

Without acceptance there can be no compromise. Without acceptance we have little room for anything but our idealized notions of the way things "should" be, and this rigidity makes us impenetrable. But when we start to find our way to acceptance, these barriers begin dissolving. We start to experience humanness in others, as well as ourselves, and what once seemed non-negotiable suddenly seems possible. She doesn't *have* to be a redhead or younger than you are; he doesn't have to be six feet tall, or even taller than you are. She doesn't have to be a vegetarian; he doesn't have to love travel. With acceptance we start appreciating different ways of being, looking, feeling, thinking, and acting.

With acceptance we start appreciating different ways of being, looking, feeling, thinking, and acting.

One thing I continue to marvel at in my own relationship is how my growing capacity for acceptance has opened doors to compromise. When my relationship requirements were narrow and rigid, there was no real road to finding middle ground. Frankly, I didn't even understand what healthy compromise was. It's incredible how much energy—and anger—I often invested in keeping myself separate and uncompromising. But when I started to find more room for differences, when that need to be difficult and closed off started to dissolve, I suddenly found myself negotiating in new and productive ways. Yes, there were moments of frustration and even anger, but I no longer felt as though I was selling my soul if I deviated one iota from my entrenched positions. As I became more and more capable of meeting my partner halfway, I was also able to experience what it felt like to have a partner who was also willing to meet me halfway. And I quickly grew to appreciate how wonderful it is to be with someone who cares more about preserving the relationship than she does about taking a stand.

In a loving relationship, one quickly learns to accept that you can't always have exactly what you want when you want it. That does not mean that the relationship is flawed. It simply means that you and your partner are two different and unique people who are trying to stay connected.

The Courage to Define a New Path

I firmly believe that each of us has the power and the capacity to find the love and commitment we want. But we have to start doing things differently. The failure to make good choices has taken too many of us into relationships that have been (to frame these relationships in the most positive way) "rich with lessons." These "love lessons" are exhausting. I remember so many times thinking to myself, "Enough lessons! I want a life!" On the way to finally getting the life I wanted, I eventually managed to learn a surprisingly simple, but essential, lesson:

No one can have a satisfying relationship until he or she is ready to behave in new and better ways.

In short, clearing out the old makes room for the new.

Don't we all have tired and worn-out behavior patterns that need to be shed? Take Glen, for example. When Glen was an insecure thirteen-year-old, he would try to get a girl to notice him by showing off his well-practiced belching techniques. Now Glen is thirty, and he regularly goes to bars to meet women. While he has stopped the belching, he hasn't stopped showing off. Watch his behavior, and you see that he is just as obnoxious now as he was at thirteen. Of course Glen is having some success with women, but is he having success with the women he really likes? Of course not. Why doesn't he see what he is doing? If he became more aware of what he is doing, wouldn't he be able to change his lame-brained behavior? If we all became more aware of what we are doing, wouldn't we be able to change some of our own ineffective patterns?

Some of the ways we behave in the course of trying to develop a lasting love are the products of complex programming and other sophisticated psychological mechanisms that require time, energy, and considerable motivation to explore, understand, and alter. But there are many, many things we do out of habit—things we do over and over and over again, often for no reason other than their familiarity and comfort value.

We have practiced these behaviors for so many years of our lives, through so many different relationships, that they feel like a part of who we are. We don't question them. We don't try to understand them. We don't consider their usefulness. We don't consider the fallout they create. We don't ever think about changing them. And it's hard to imagine that they may be getting in the way of our chances for lasting connection and commitment. But they are. They are a huge obstacle. And that's the bad news. The good news is that many of these behaviors are relatively simple to change. And that you can start changing some right now.

we do things over and over and over again, often for no reason other than their familiarity

Changing self-defeating habits begins by becoming a skilled observer of your relationships, both past and present, and a skilled observer of yourself in these relationships. You need to be able to see patterns in your choices and your behaviors. And you need to be able to see your self-defeating responses.

When we elect to be completely "unconscious" about our relationships, every partner feels new and different, and every experience feels new and different. When a relationship ends we try to split it off from our active memory and tuck it away in a place where it won't trouble us. And when we start again, we think we are starting fresh.

But when we elect to "wake up," we quickly begin to see a different picture—a picture full of common threads. Sometimes we can see so many common threads it suddenly seems as though we are always wearing the same clothes. The "uniqueness" of our many relationship experiences becomes questionable. In fact, sometimes our relationships begin to look as though they were cranked out by a Xerox machine.

For most of my adult life I have been an observer of relationships. It is how I have made my living, and it is how I like to look at the world. But I must admit that the very last relationships I came to observe were my own. I wanted to think that each experience was unique, that each partner was unique, and that I was new and different each time. I had no interest in looking too carefully. I had no interest in learning from the past (frankly, I didn't believe that I could). All that concerned me was "the next one." As you might imagine, when I finally did stop and turn one eye inward, the experience was truly humbling. It was also very helpful.

What I learned very quickly was that I did have some control over the way I conducted myself in relationships. While I could not magically make my fears dissolve, I could lessen their intensity and their impact. So many of my knee-jerk behaviors were creating unnecessary pressure, sending inappropriate messages, and setting up potential partners (as well as myself) for hurt or disappointment. And all I had to do to change this was to stop that knee from jerking. I think you can do this too.

SHEDDING RELATIONSHIP HABITS THAT SABOTAGE CONNECTION

The following list of self-defeating relationship habits and knee-jerk reactions comes from years of watching and learning. But this list is by no means inclusive, it is intended only to start you on your way. Your greatest insights will come from your own commitment (there is that word again) to observing yourself in your world. From questioning your motives. From questioning your strategies. From questioning your magical thinking. From questioning your behaviors. From questioning your choices. Even from questioning why you don't ask enough questions.

It may seem like I'm trying to take all of the fun out of relationships by asking you to put so much of your life under a magnifying glass. But what I am really doing is trying to give you the tools to set you free, so you can move more easily and successfully in the direction of committed partnership.

SAY GOOD-BYE TO TYPE CASTING

Is there a "type" of person that you're always looking for? Do you fail to notice anyone, no matter how appropriate, who doesn't conform to that description? Do you have friends and family trained to "be on the lookout" for someone who is your type, and have them so well-programmed that they don't even think of you as a possibility when they come across a different "type"? Does he have to be tall, dark, and handsome before you would consider him? Or short, fair-haired, and muscular? Does she have to be petite and blonde? Or tall and leggy with long hair? Maybe you're always looking for the professorial type. Or the dressed-for-success go-getter. Or the energetic cheerleader. Or the tortured artist. Or the man or woman with a host of personal problems. Whatever your type is, it's time to break the mold. And the sooner you do it, the better.

There is a huge difference between being *partial* to a certain look, or style, or energy, and being a slave to that type. When someone *has* to be your type, it keeps you from experiencing people as individuals. It also discourages others from helping you in your search. And it minimizes your chances for finding a valuable connection because it puts so many unnecessary constraints on your world. This is not the profile of a person who is open to real relationship.

You could probably guess from what I have already told you about myself that I wasted many good years of my life trying to "type cast" my relationships. One friend of mine, who actually knew my wife two years before I did, never considered setting the two of us up because he didn't think she fit the profile I had imprinted upon his brain! Very luckily, I met my wife anyway, but I could have just as easily missed the opportunity. Think about the opportunities *you* may be missing right now. Now think about how you can start opening yourself up to those opportunities by changing the way you approach possibility, and changing the messages you choose to give to the world.

If you are reading this book, in all probability your type has not worked for you in the past. Why do you expect it to be different in the future? Take some chances, make some compromises, and see what happens.

GIVE UP FEARLESS PURSUIT

When Ed meets someone, he will say or do practically anything to make her respond. He writes shamelessly gushy poetry; he hires an airplane to fly a banner saying "I love you!" across the sky; he tells her that she is the most important person in his life.

Ed's sister, Edwina, has a different style, but with many of the same results. When she meets a man she likes, she turns him into her project: She flirts outrageously; she sends cute, sexy faxes or notes; she sends adorable little presents; she tells him that he is the smartest, best-looking person she has ever met; she tells him that he is the best lover she has ever known.

Neither Ed nor Edwina know how to take no for an answer. They are determined; they are driven. And their actions appear absolutely fearless. But guess what, they are not fearless. Quite the contrary, they are full of fear. And experience should remind them that their fear will surface as soon as they have made the conquest. So they are really being incredibly dishonest. And they are also setting up the classic pursuit and panic scenario.

It's easy to be fearless at the beginning of a relationship. It's easy to immerse yourself in your feelings while failing to consider the consequences of what you are doing. Reckless pursuit is part of a fantasy style, and it's a destructive pattern.

When we embrace the larger picture, and decide to be more accountable for our actions and their consequences, we start thinking very differently about the style of our pursuit. We begin to see that well-intentioned people can suffer terribly by misinterpreting our words and actions; we are far more inclined to take the initial phases of relationship a lot more seriously and responsibly. In this way, regardless of the ultimate outcome, many painful feelings can be spared.

If we had no fear of commitment, it might be charming to be so aggressive when pursuing new partners. Not necessary, of course, but possibly somewhat charming. Given a certain level of fear, however, it simply isn't fair. A façade of fearlessness will always backfire one of two ways. It will scare away any partner who is grounded and appropriately cautious, and it will unfairly seduce anyone who has been silently hoping for love at first sight. Either way, someone is always getting hurt. This cannot be what you want, but it is certainly what you are creating. Yet it doesn't have to be this way. You do have choices.

You can start, for example, by being more authentic and presenting a picture that is more congruent with who you really are in relationships: someone who isn't fearless at all. You can proceed cautiously, with the smallest steps, and work with your fears as they slowly surface. Instead of acting like an out-of-control Mack truck, you can ride the brake like a "slow moving vehicle" and embrace the timeless lesson of the tortoise and the hare. It may not sound very sexy or exciting to you. But it is honest. And it is your best chance of ever reaching the destination you desire.

RECOGNIZE GOOD SALESMANSHIP FOR WHAT IT IS

He wines and dines you in the finest restaurants and showers you with gifts. You've only just met, yet he spends hours helping you take your dog to the vet. He sings you songs and fills your refrigerator with his own homemade rice pudding. And that's just about all it takes to have you lower your defenses and open your heart. Your thinking goes something like this: "He must like me to give me so much attention." When it should really be going like this: "He probably does this with *every* woman."

You just met, yet she arrives at your door today looking unbelievably attractive in a blue work shirt and offers to help you paint your apartment. She invites you to spend the night at her house, even though you've only known her for three days. And that's just about all it takes to have you spinning scenarios of a long future together. Your thinking goes something like this: "She must be really crazy about me to want to have sex so quickly." When it should really be going like this: "She must be able to compartmentalize her sex life if she can get physically intimate this quickly with a relative stranger."

Every single one of us wants to feel special. And many of us want to feel that we alone have been chosen to be the object of someone's most profound affections—particularly when that someone seems attractive and desirable. It's so easy to be seduced by a hard sell, and it's understandable. But that doesn't make it wise. If there is one thing you should never let yourself trust in a new relationship, it is the experience of "too much, too fast." If you are the one who is doing all the rushing, you need to be examining your motives. And if you are on the receiving end of this whirlwind, it should put you on your guard immediately.

While your desire to feel special may be clouding your judgment, I know that you still have good instincts somewhere inside you warning that all is not quite right. You need to reconnect with those more protective instincts before you come to any conclusions about what all of this seductive behavior is about. Maybe it *is* a sign that something unusual and special is happening this time. But it is far more likely to be a crucial sign that you can't make *any* assumptions about this relationship. It's fine to enjoy the attention. Just don't confuse intense short-term attention with serious long-term intentions.

DON'T LET FANTASIES LEAD YOU AWAY FROM REAL LOVE

Every time you see an attractive stranger you wonder, "Could this be the one?" Consequently you spend hours and hours of your precious time creating daydreams about people you barely know. You let your thoughts of television personalities get out of hand; you dream about professional athletes; you chase attractive strangers down the street; you behave bizarrely in order to get yourself noticed by someone you don't know in the hopes of having a single conversation; you spend months trying to get to meet somebody who works elsewhere in your office building—even when you don't know if this person is available. Many times your efforts fail and you are left in a state of longing and grieving. But even if your efforts pay off, and you manage to actually make an initial connection, it doesn't take long before you are feeling disappointed. And though you may not even notice it, you are wasting a lot of time.

What is it that you are looking for? What is it you are hoping to find? Experience tells me that it's not really a person you are chasing down the street, it is a *feeling* that you are after. That magical feeling so many of us are desperate to find is the feeling of "perfect connection" that exists only in our dreams. There is no *real* connection that can feel this complete. There is no *real* person who has this much magic. Your experience has already confirmed this for you again and again and again. When are you going to try to find the strength to integrate this knowledge into your behavior?

Most of us who are looking for that feeling of perfect merger are looking for a feeling we lost very early in life—in infancy, or early childhood. And the place to come to terms with that loss is in the office of a trained therapist or counselor who can help you put those pieces of your past together. No partner can be expected to make up for that loss, but there are plenty of partners who still have lots of love to offer. Don't keep turning your back on these real people, and their real love, because you are determined to find something all-consuming and larger than life.

START ACTIVELY—AND APPROPRIATELY—LOOKING FOR LOVE

You say that you want love and commitment, but you're waiting for it to knock on your door. You spend your life waiting for love to find you, and you don't even bother to make yourself available. You don't ask friends to set you up. You don't know how to circulate. Not only do you not know how to flirt, you don't want to even try. You don't know how to pursue the kind of partners you are interested in. You don't make conversation with the people you meet casually. You don't make eye contact. You don't do anything to actively meet people. So who finds you? Only the hardened professionals—Don Juans or Juanitas who are challenged by your defense system. Once you respond, however, their heated pursuit almost inevitably turns into heated panic.

When you need a job you go out and get yourself a job, even if it means reading ads, networking, and knocking on doors. You do it in an intelligent, well-thought-out manner that maximizes what you have to offer. And you make it happen. So why won't you do everything you can to make commitment happen? You need to assume more of your own power and start stepping up to the plate. It's not always easy and it's not always fun, and yes, there will be many times when you wish you were home watching mediocre television. But it gives you a fighting chance to get what you want.

This is not a suggestion to race out right now to your favorite single's bar or disco. We'll talk about that bad habit in just a moment. But it is an invitation to take more control of your romantic future. The princess-in-the-ivory-tower approach is a worthless vestige from your third-grade reading list, and a habit you need to break. Being the "waiter" is a wonderful way to always keep yourself from being in a position of power. You have choices here.

STOP LOOKING FOR LOVE IN ALL THE WRONG PLACES

Janelle says she can never find a guy who wants to take the time to talk and get to know her, even though she meets new guys almost every week at her favorite dance club, which has to be the noisiest place in North America. Andrew, who is thirty-two, says that none of the women he meets are serious about relationships. Yet the only places he goes are the bars and restaurants located adjacent to the local university in his home town. Victoria, who only dates "guys in the business" (show business, that is), complains that the men she meets are shallow, narcissistic, and only interested in getting better parts. Kevin has asked everyone he knows to help him "find blind dates," but he has also said that he could only be interested in a woman who is very, very pretty. They are afraid to introduce Kevin to anyone. They worry that Kevin will make any woman feel as though she can't measure up to his expectations. Consequently Kevin's friends haven't come through.

What's wrong here? Everything. If you want to find better prospects for long-term love, you need to start prospecting with some intelligence. Where are people with your values, your goals, and your interest in a committed relationship most likely to be found? What is the appropriate age range? What are their likely professions? Where might you meet them in an atmosphere that is conducive to the beginnings of a genuine connection? Within the last six months, for example, I've spoken to three people who started serious relationships at high school or college reunions. Yet when I suggest reunions as one example of a good place to connect or reconnect, inevitably people look at me as though I'm out of touch with the real world. Some very smart people play very dumb when they play the meeting game, and then they are surprised or disappointed when it backfires. Take a long hard look at your selection strategies, or complete lack thereof, and consider how you might make some productive adjustments to these old, unproductive habits.

DON'T SET YOURSELF UP FOR TROUBLE BY SELLING YOURSELF OUT

When he is dating a potential new partner, Tom always acts as though money is no object. He doesn't want to appear to be cheap, because he isn't. He doesn't want to appear to be poor, because he isn't. He doesn't want to appear "unromantic," because he is very romantic. He doesn't want to be judged according to what he has or doesn't have. He just doesn't want money issues to get in the way in the very beginning of a relationship. Yet Tom is actually on a very limited budget because his income is stable, but modest, and if the relationship starts to "click" Tom starts to panic because he knows he can't keep up his easy-spending façade.

> **Many of us will do anything we can to get a partner interested and to cement the connection**

Like Tom, Summer hides the full picture of who she is when she is beginning a relationship. If the guy she is seeing is also seeing other women, she tells him it's "no problem." If the guy she is seeing says he is having a hard time saying goodbye to his ex-girlfriend, she tells him, "take your time." Summer feels she needs to appear to be understanding and patient, but she doesn't really feel this way at all inside. Inside she is silently stewing, waiting for these other women to go away. But they don't seem to ever go away, and Summer ends up with relationships she can't live with.

In the beginning of a relationship, many of us will do anything we can to get a partner interested and cement the connection, even if that means seriously compromising who we are. We hide the truth about our financial status. We hide the truth about our emotional status. We may even hide our kids. We don't defend our values, we don't voice our true opinions, and we don't speak up for our needs. And we think we are doing the right thing.

But if you can't live with the picture you are painting of yourself, then you are not doing the right thing. Quite the contrary, you are setting yourself up for anger, resentment, panic, or pain. You think you're just trying to not make waves, but by "holding the water back" now, when you are less vested in the relationship, you are insuring that gigantic waves—tidal waves—will come crashing down later when you have a lot more to lose. It doesn't add up to be an intelligent strategy if commitment is truly your goal.

DON'T TURN YOUR RELATIONSHIP INTO THERAPY

Some of us seem to be drawn toward relationships in which we almost inevitably fall into the role of either a therapist or a patient. Ted, for example, is truly conflicted about whether he wants his relationship with Katie to continue. He feels ripped apart. And with whom does he choose to share his angst? Why with Katie of course. He treats Katie as though she is his therapist. She's a good listener; she finds the details of Ted's psyche all-engrossing; and she seems to genuinely understand's Ted's problem.

The relationship right now has become wildly lopsided. It's all about what Ted wants, what Ted needs, what Ted fears. Ted doesn't understand how incredibly selfish he is being. He isn't even thinking about whether or not Katie should have to listen to his internal dialogue or the sometimes harsh evaluation that goes hand in hand with his ambivalence. Ted also doesn't understand that his actions, in a peculiar way, have given Katie a false sense of hope. To Katie, his attitude says, "I want you to be a part of my struggle because it's *our* struggle." To Katie, his words imply, "I want *us* to work this out for *us.*" But that's not necessarily how Ted feels.

If Ted sincerely wants to bring Katie more fully into his head to understand his internal struggle with commitment, he should be doing it in a therapist's office—as opposed to treating Katie as though she *is* the therapist. Katie needs an interpreter to help her understand what's taking place. And Ted needs a referee—someone who can make him more fully accountable for his words and actions. They both need someone to help them set boundaries. This is what a therapist is paid to do.

If you're ever in a relationship in which you are playing the role of either therapist or patient, recognize that the relationship needs professional help.

IF YOUR PARTNER STARTS GIVING YOU LESS, DON'T AUTOMATICALLY RESPOND BY GIVING MORE

She shows less interest, you respond by trying harder to show her that you are loving, lovable, and special. He says he's still not ready to be monogamous, you tell him that you'll wait patiently and monogamously. She becomes distant, you try harder and harder to get close. He becomes critical, you try to change the things he doesn't seem to care for. What's wrong with this picture? For starters: The *direction* of your responses.

Trying to give more when you are getting less is a classic knee-jerk reaction to problems in a relationship. And I know that what makes it so easy to jerk that knee is that you think you are doing the right thing. You think that your partner needs more reinforcement, more displays of your caring, more proof of your value. But it is my experience that what he/she really needs is some time alone.

Habits like this tend to start when we are very small and vulnerable in the presence of people we love. Someone who is special to us expresses their disapproval, and we try harder to get approval. Someone who is special to us has no time for us, and we try harder to get noticed. Someone who is special to us criticizes us, and we try harder to please. That "someone" was probably a parent, caretaker, or sibling who was trying to control the way you behaved. But today it is not a control issue you are dealing with; you are dealing with a lover/partner who is fearfully trying to back away. These are different circumstances. Your partner has a very different motivation here and it calls for a very different response. This is not a test of your caring or your love. This person is trying to take away what he/she has given you, and the appropriate response is for you to back away also and immediately start giving as little, or even less, than you are now being given. This is the only response that will keep you from feeling powerless.

When situations like this arise, it helps to have a compass and to know how to read it. If he suddenly pulls away and starts heading west, you need to head east. If she is eyeing the south, you should be eyeing the north. Your appropriate responses will help keep your partner's sudden swings in check, and keep you grounded and sane in the midst of behaviors that are not at all grounded or loving.

KEEP YOUR LIVES SEPARATE UNTIL YOU'RE SURE YOUR HEARTS ARE JOINED

Scenario #1: You're spending way too much time on the phone. The drive to his/her house is knocking you out. If you spend the night at his/her house, you never have the right clothes for work the next day. You're feeling frustrated much of the time. So why not try to live together, and make everything more simple? After all, it's the '90s.

Scenario #2: You're both interested in the same line of work. Perhaps you can be working on a project together? Or starting a small company together? Or giving this person a job? Sure, you've only known each other for a couple of months, but it could be such a productive merger. And it could be so romantic. Why not give it a shot?

Let me try to give you a clear "why not": because these physical mergers tend to backfire by putting too much pressure on a budding relationship. Here's another "why not": because there is nothing more painful and costly than having to undo this physical merger if your emotional merger never comes to fruition.

I can't begin to tell you how many people I know who are in unhappy relationships that became serious too quickly. Healthy relationships come together the way a jig-saw puzzle comes together: one tiny piece at a time. It's a process, a slow process, and you have to live through it. Living together works when both partners are committed to making it work, but that commitment only comes when emotional connections are firm. Do you have that commitment? Do you have those connections? Or are you just hoping they will magically appear from living under the same roof, or working under the same roof. They don't. One has nothing to do with the other, and one cannot "force" the other. So before you uproot your life, your partner's life, your children's lives, your pet's life, buy real estate together, start a business together, or commit yourself to a working relationship, how about committing yourself to *taking your time?*

ONLY MAKE PROMISES WHEN YOU'RE SURE YOU CAN KEEP THEM

You tell her that you can't wait till she meets your family. You tell him that you can't wait till he meets your best friend. You tell her you want to take her to Europe. You tell him you can't wait to spend the summer together. You tell her that she makes you think about marriage. You tell him that he makes you think about raising a family. You tell her that you always want to be together. You tell him that you can see him as always being a part of your life. Promises, promises, promises. And you've only known each other a few weeks. Is any of this future talk really necessary? Is any of it really helpful? The answer is no.

There's only one promise you need to make in the beginning of a relationship: a promise to yourself to give the relationship your best shot. You don't need to promise a new partner anything. And you are both much better off if you don't. "Future talk" is incredibly seductive, and it is a perfect setup for disappointment and hurt. Making promises suggests that you are already clear about your commitment for the future. And people tend to trust what you are saying, and even start planning their lives around what you are saying. But you aren't clear about your commitment. You can't be. Not in the beginning of a relationship. You may be clear that you are having very intense feelings, and these feelings may be leading you to fantasize about the future, but these are only fantasies. And they are fantasies you have to keep to yourself, until you really *can* make a commitment.

DON'T BE AFRAID TO ASK YOUR PROSPECTIVE PARTNERS A LOT OF QUESTIONS

Sometimes we have BIG reasons for not asking questions. We're afraid to hear the answers. Or we're afraid to make a scene. Or we're afraid our potential partner will turn around and ask us the very same questions, and we know that our answers will not be well received. So we don't ask, and we live with the consequences.

But sometimes there are no big reasons for not asking questions. It's just a bad habit you have, stemming from a very naive sense that people will involuntarily tell you, or that you will be able to intuit everything you need to know. Or it's a bad habit you have stemming from an equally naive sense that you can never get that hurt.

Sure, maybe you don't want to pry, or make anyone uncomfortable. But people expect to be asked a lot of questions about their relationship history, their hopes, and their intentions. People expect to be asked about their family and their work. And if someone seems to be discouraging you from asking, all the more reason you need to ask.

It is the absence of information that sets the stage for such horrible relationship surprises, surprises such as, "I can't believe he didn't tell me he was married!" Or "I can't believe she didn't tell me she had a kid!" Or "I can't believe he didn't tell me he would never get married again!" Or "I can't believe she didn't tell me she has never been faithful to a partner!" Or "I can't believe he didn't tell me that he wasn't looking for a committed relationship!" Does any of this sound familiar?

When you meet someone new, make a list of things you will need to know before you completely open your heart. And your list should naturally expand as the relationship progresses. You don't have to have all these questions answered on your first phone call (and it would probably be better if you didn't, unless you have a very short list). But you do need these answers sooner, rather than later, to help you gauge short-term possibilities, long-term possibilities, and overall risks.

STOP COMMITTING YOURSELF TO THE UNAVAILABLE PARTNERS

He tells you he could never leave his wife. He tells you he's moving to Australia. He tells you he has six months to live. He tells you he wants to travel the world *alone*. She tells you she's still in love with her ex. She tells you she could never fall in love with a man. She tells you she has a real problem with commitment. And while any of these honest admissions should be more than enough to send you on your way, instead they capture your interest. Next thing you know, you have completely committed yourself to the uncommittable, and you are prepared to invest months or years trying to make this love work.

Does it sound like I am exaggerating here? I wish I were, but I'm not. I have personally seen scenarios just like these acted out hundreds of times, I have heard about hundreds more, and they never cease to amaze me. Men and women who know from the very beginning that they are in an impossible situation, but choose to commit themselves to this impossible situation one thousand and one percent. And then they say, "look at me . . . look at how much I can commit!"

When I encounter this very convoluted scenario I only have one question for the participant: If you are completely committed to the uncommittable are you really committed at all . . . or have you just found a very clever way to avoid any prospect of real commitment? I think you know my answer to this question. I only hope you have the courage to believe me and start making different choices.

STOP GOING FROM PARTNER TO PARTNER, BELIEVING THAT YOU WILL BE SAVED BY SOMEONE ELSE'S LOVE

Tammy's relationship history looks something like this:

Tammy met Billy and fell in love. They were together until Billy broke Tammy's heart. Tammy nursed her broken heart until she fell in love with Jake. Eventually Jake left Tammy for somebody else, and Tammy became very depressed and stayed that way until she met and fell in love with Colin ...

Billy's relationship history looks something like this:

He fell in love with Rhonda, but he began to feel unhappy with the relationship, and while they were still going out, he met Patti, which ended his relationship with Rhonda. His relationship with Patti ended because he met Grace, and his relationship with Grace ended when he fell overboard for Frieda, who dumped him for somebody else. Billy was heartsick for approximately twenty-four hours before he started his pattern all over again with June ...

Although it would appear that Tammy and Billy are very different (after all Tammy experiences great difficulty recovering from the end of a relationship while Billy spends almost no time in recovery), they both follow the same premise. They both believe that a new partner is going to resolve their old pain and confusion. It doesn't work this way.

If any of us wants to get to a satisfying committed relationship, we need to first experience our own strength in the absence of partnership. We need to learn more about the healing process and appropriate grieving. Yes, love does heal, but if we make the mistake of believing that someone else's love is the way to salvation, there will be a constant sense of desperation to our actions; we will inevitably feel as though we have no real power in our relationships.

Here are some suggestions for handling the end of a relationship:

1. Take at least a month to process and come to terms with what happened before you do anything else.
2. Use this time to fortify the relationship that you have with yourself. Try to find things that you will enjoy. Work at building your independence. Enjoy your friends. Don't obsess about what happened, and don't isolate yourself from people who care about you.
3. If several months have passed, and you are still haunted by the grieving, recognize that new losses trigger emotional memories of old losses and they all become bundled. This can be overwhelming without the help of some professional counseling. The good news is that these times provide opportunities to heal losses, both old and new.

KEEP YOUR RELATIONSHIPS FIXED IN THE PRESENT TENSE

Barbara met Terrance last night. In her head, she is already thinking about what their babies might look like.

Buddy has been going out with Glynis for two weeks. He likes her a lot, but he can't stop worrying about what will happen to the relationship if he and his best friend take the summer vacation they planned.

Many people sabotage their relationships because they don't allow themselves to enjoy what they have at that moment. As soon as they start feeling comfortable in a relationship, they sabotage that comfort by time-traveling into the future to their confused picture of what the relationship might become. I know that I've done this. Sure, everything is fine right now, I would say to myself, but what would things be like if we stayed together? I would do this automatically, never understanding that the reason I could so easily shift my focus to all these future concerns was that everything was working so well in the moment. The relationship had potential. Things were basically good. So I immediately started searching for a place where I would not be comfortable: thirty, forty, or fifty years into the future. And I started painting pictures of how "not good" things might get. This was a hideous habit that completely undermined my ability to enjoy what I had, as well as any chance of actually reaching that future.

When a relationship is in its infancy, the focus of that relationship should be in the present. You must be doing everything you can to maximize your sense of connectedness in the moment. And if you are going to be asking yourself questions, they should be questions such as, "How do I feel being with this person?" "Is this person being kind and honest?" "Am I being open and honest?" "Are we getting along, and if not, why not?"

Of course you need to be concerned about the future of the relationship if you start seeing red flags that warn you of potential problems such as infidelity, abusive patterns, or commitment conflicts. And it is not inappropriate to be wondering about the potential that exists for something loving and long term. But what you should *not* be obsessing about are neurotic "future issues"—unanswerable issues—such as, "What will she/he look like in thirty years?" "Will he gain too much weight?" "Will she have a double chin?" "Will we be attracted to each other when we get old?" "Will we fight all the time?" "Will I still find other women attractive?" There are no real answers to questions like this in the present, and trying to make your own answers now will only confuse and mislead you. I have said this already but I'm going to say it once again. Relationships evolve hour by hour and day by day. And that is where all of your attention, energy, and efforts should be. You must give everything you have to each of the moments you have together, and you must savor the experience. You must be *in* the relationship. Every time you jump light years into the future, you are leaving reality, the relationship, and the connection behind.

> **Many people sabotage their relationships because they don't allow themselves to enjoy what they have at that moment.**

Getting a Handle on Your Patterns

Perhaps you have identified with many of these patterns, and seen yourself in too many of these scenarios. This has not been a test and there is nothing to be ashamed of here. To the contrary, your willingness to see yourself in these descriptions reflects considerable courage. And it also tells me you are ready for change.

If these habits were fairly harmless, it wouldn't really matter what you did or did not do on the road to finding love. But they are not harmless at all, they are actually quite destructive. Sometimes we are setting up people who care about us to experience confusion, disappointment, and hurt. Other times we are setting ourselves up for the same painful array. Either way, true commitment never comes.

It is one thing to practice knee-jerk behaviors and habits when we are unaware of our patterns and unaware of the consequences. But now you are aware of those patterns and you are aware of those consequences. So the time has come to do things differently, and do them in the service of long-term commitment goals. Your old relationship habits and behaviors have damaged your capacity to connect with integrity and have kept you stuck for too long. It is time to move forward. It is time to "kick" these habits and start connecting from the heart. Are you up for the challenge? I think you are. Because I know you have the courage.

During my many years of trying and failing to make love work, I felt that change was not possible. But that is partially because I never questioned my behaviors or challenged habits I had become comfortable with. Today, having real love in my life, I have learned that change *is* possible. And it can start for you today by committing yourself to break old habits and build healthier possibilities.

CHALLENGE EIGHT

The Courage to Handle Your Anxieties

*G*reg and Miranda are sitting together in an urban coffee shop. They are both drinking cappuccino. It is a Sunday morning in mid-December. Last night in honor of their one-month anniversary, they had sex for the first time. It was awkward, as sex for the first time so often is. But it also felt intimate and loving. Could this be the beginning of a committed relationship? Both of their heads are filled with hundreds of jumbled thoughts.

For example:

- Does this mean he/she's going to be expecting that we spend New Year's Eve together? I made those plans to go skiing with my friends weeks ago. I can't change them now. But I don't want him/her to find somebody else because I'm not around. Should I say something about it or should I just wait?
- Christmas is just next week. Should I buy a present? How much should I spend? I don't want it to be such an important gift that I'll be embarrassed if he/she doesn't have a present for me, but I also don't want to look as though I'm cheap or have bad taste.
- Am I really ready for the "real thing"? I wanted to date for a few more years. I wonder what he/she expects.
- I wonder if he/she noticed my love handles? I wonder if he/she still finds me attractive? I wonder if I did something last night that turned him/her off? What can I say in order to find out?
- Maybe one of us should make our intentions clear. What are my intentions anyway?

- I shouldn't have eaten that garlic shrimp last night. My breath must really stink.
- She seems a little more withdrawn than she did last night. Does that mean she can't wait to get away? I noticed the way she looked at that good-looking waiter in the restaurant last night. Maybe I'm not really her type.
- He's looking at his watch. Where does he want to go? Does he have another date? He stares at every long-legged woman who walks by. If this relationship goes anywhere, will I always be thinking about my thighs?

All of these thoughts reflect a certain amount of anxiety, don't they. Relationships and anxiety often seem to go hand in hand. This is particularly true in new relationships. For better or worse, it is the way love works. But as we struggle to fall in love and stay in love, we all have at least a few "hair-triggers." Some of us become anxious because we fear rejection; some of us become anxious because we feel crowded. Sometimes we become anxious because we fear for ourselves; sometimes we become anxious because we worry about those we love. Often anxiety is simply a sign that we care and that the relationship has real possibilities.

> **Often anxiety is simply a sign that we care and that the relationship has real possibilities.**

We would all be happier if someone were able to give us accurate information about what to do and what the future will bring. We want someone to provide meaningful, soothing, all-knowing explanations for each wave of anxiety as it surfaces. In the absence of such a higher omniscient authority to tell us what our partner is thinking, we can easily become confused, agitated, or insecure. We want to know what our partners think and feel; we want to be able to respond appropriately. Without this information, too often our anxieties take over. They dominate our thinking and inevitably end up playing too large a role in the course a relationship will or will not take.

ANXIOUS FROM RELATIONSHIP DAY # 1

Laura recently went to a party where she met a man named Scott who seemed very attracted to her. Although Laura wasn't sure she liked him, she gave him her number and, at his request, her e-mail address. The next morning when she woke up and turned on her computer, she had e-mail from Scott; it included several jokes going around the net. Very funny. Scott followed up by calling her the next day. And the next. And the next. Flattered, but still somewhat reluctant, Laura agreed to meet him for dinner on Saturday night.

As Saturday approached, Laura found that her enthusiasm was growing. She enjoyed going through the little rituals of preparing for a Saturday night date, and she began to think about how nice it would be to have somebody to go out with. Then, over dinner, Laura began to see things about Scott that she liked. He was funny. He was smart. And his most appealing quality, as far as she was concerned, was how much he seemed to like her. His interest in her was very persuasive. "Why," she thought to herself, "shouldn't I be with someone who likes me more than I like him?"

Scott took Laura home, and they began to kiss in front of her door. Long, lingering kisses. "Very, very nice!" Laura thought. Scott finally left, saying he would call. Laura wasn't sure what that meant. She sort of expected him to call Sunday or Monday just to say hello, but he didn't. By Wednesday night, Laura was getting anxious. She wondered whether she should make plans for Saturday or save the night for Scott. She worried that he wouldn't call at all. She wondered if she had done something to turn him off over dinner. She even considered calling him. How does this happen? She asks herself. She barely knows Scott, and yet *she finds herself waiting for the phone to ring!*

When Scott finally called on Saturday morning and asked her out for Sunday afternoon, Laura's immediate reaction was relief. Then she began to worry whether or not she had been "demoted." Why didn't he ask her out for Saturday night? Why is this happening? If Laura searched her true feelings, she would have to acknowledge that she isn't even sure if she likes or is attracted to Scott. However, Laura's anxieties about the future of their relationship are so intense that they automatically give Scott power over her life.

This is how Laura is with relationships. And it's no fun!

Why Do Relationships Make Laura Feel Anxious and out of Control?

It's no secret that by assuming an active and more aggressive role, men have culturally controlled the dating process and the speed with which relationships begin. It's no secret that the old-fashioned traditional dating structure—boy pursues girl—has left women feeling powerless and out of control. Waiting for a man you like, or anybody else, to phone can be anxiety provoking; waiting to find out whether you pass muster is anxiety provoking. Men, of course, also become anxious wondering whether a woman will say yes or no. But, it is different. As a man I grew up knowing that I didn't have to wait for someone else to "select" me. I was the "selector," and there is no question that it's the better position.

In Laura's case, this traditional pattern has been reinforced by her own background. The losses and ghosts in her life have left her ultra sensitive. From all outward appearances, there is no reason to believe that relationships should make Laura anxious. She has an intact family with two loving parents. However Laura's mother became ill when Laura was very small and was often hospitalized for extended periods of time; Laura remembers worrying whether her mother would ever return. During these years, Laura's father had a very discreet affair with his secretary—something Laura only discovered within the last few years. Now that Laura knows this, she is beginning to understand some of the messages her mother subtly imparted over the years about how men were fickle and not totally trustworthy. Laura's parents gave her two other messages: They told Laura that having a relationship is the most important thing in life; they also told her that she is so beautiful and smart that someday a man would come along who would immediately see how wonderful she is.

Laura's various high school and college romances began to compound some of these messages. Unlike many of her friends, Laura always had a difficult time letting go when a romance ended. She was never able to date casually or go from person to person. She was always surprised by male behavior; she always expected her relationships to be serious; and she had several disappointments. These experiences left Laura feeling hurt and despondent. She would stay that way until she met somebody new, and then the process would begin all over again.

By the time Laura met Scott, she was completely sensitized. If Scott doesn't call when he says he will, Laura will immediately assume the worse: *He already has a girlfriend. She was out of town; now she's back... or... He has met someone else. He no longer likes me. He doesn't want me. I'm losing him.*

And What About Scott?

Scott is lonely. He's always been lonely. Although he was raised by a doting mother, his father was often absent for long periods; even worse, Scott's father was often too angry to get close to even when he was home. Scott always felt his family was different than the families of his friends; and although he was popular and a good athlete, he never really felt as though he fit in.

Scott got married within weeks of his college graduation, but he knew as he was doing it that it was a mistake that he would later regret. He and his wife were good friends and buddies, but there wasn't very much passion. Fortunately his wife didn't become pregnant, and after five years they both realized that they wanted more. Scott began dating furiously. It was a different world; he was older and more secure. He had a good job; he had nice clothes; he had his own place. And there were so many women to date.

However, Scott never really seemed able to just date. When he didn't have a girlfriend, he devoted all of his energy to finding one. And with almost every woman he dated, things always got serious. With these women Scott always finds himself revealing too much about himself and saying things he later regrets. Remember Scott is lonely. He wants connection. But he's not at all sure about this commitment business. He's been single now for six years, and his conflict keeps getting him into trouble with women.

With Laura, Scott's already afraid of more of the same. At first, he was anxious about whether or not she'd agree to go out with him. When she finally said yes, he was anxious that she might cancel. And when she didn't cancel, he was afraid that she might not like him that much. So he picked a restaurant that he thought would impress her, and he knocked himself out trying to endear himself to her right away. Scott didn't relax for a second as he worked to be his most charming self.

But by the time the date ended, Scott felt his concerns shifting. It had become clear to him that all his hard work had paid off: Laura *did* like him, and she would definitely see him again if he asked. Now he had a new problem to worry about: How far did he want this relationship to go? He liked Laura. He definitely did. But how *much* did he like Laura? He wasn't really sure.

Scott started thinking about the woman he flirted with at Blockbuster Video the other night. He was sure he could "bump into her" again if he really applied himself, and she was certainly attractive too. He also found himself thinking about the coat check woman at the restaurant. When she handed Laura her coat, it was Scott who she made eye contact with. She was very cute! Was Scott ready to limit his world to *just* Laura? Scott resents having to make a decision like this right now. Why can't he just have fun? Why do things have to get serious so quickly? It doesn't help to tell Scott that Laura hasn't asked him to make any decision.

When Laura responded positively to Scott's active pursuit, it alleviated one set of Scott's anxieties, only to open up another—his "forever" anxieties. The more certain Scott is that he has the power to make Laura respond, the more he begins to question his desire to pursue things any further. Yes, Scott has been feeling very lonely. But not lonely enough, he tells himself, to give up years of his life to another wrong choice. There are so many other women, he reminds himself. And he knows he's a desirable commodity. Maybe he's just not ready. Maybe he needs to wait. At least he should slow things down and not appear like he is *too* interested right now. Two Saturday nights in a row would definitely raise her expectations and be too much. So Scott decides to shift to a Sunday, and he immediately feels relief. The problem is what will he do next week? How can he keep Laura interested without making her *too* interested. Scott's anxieties have him walking a fine line. Now that he has gotten Laura's attention, Scott finds himself wanting to be somewhat difficult—not difficult enough to completely alienate her, but difficult enough to push her back a bit.

When and How We Become Anxious

In relationships, anxiety is typically triggered whenever we fear one of the following:

- Our partner is getting too close
- Our partner is moving too far away

Not everyone, of course, has anxieties that are triggered on the first date. Many people with commitment issues stay perfectly calm and save their anxiety attacks until there is more at stake. Typically people become "anxious" at one of four different points:

1. Opening Night Jitters

A good first (or second) date makes many people anxious. One or both partners may immediately respond by believing that more is expected of him/her. The other may immediately start worrying, "Will he/she call?"

2. We Had Sex, Now What?

First-time sex also creates anxiety. Again, one partner may feel panic that he/she is expected to make a commitment, and begin to back away. In response, the other may start pressuring for greater closeness. This often sets up a vicious cycle of roles and behavior that can threaten the relationship.

3. It's Time to Get Serious

The most common point at which people get anxious is when the couple has been dating long enough for all the relationship preliminaries to be completed; it's time for the couple to move forward—together. Again, typically one partner begins to feel too much pressure and starts stalling for time. The other, also driven by anxiety, often responds with arguments and ultimatums.

4. The Morning After

Some people don't take commitment seriously until after it actually occurs (e.g., the morning after the wedding, the week after the couple moves in together or gets married). Then one or both partners may panic. He/she begins to feel crowded, have second thoughts, or becomes critical of the other.

Relationship Anxiety Is Caused by Fear. But What Are We Afraid Of?

At our jobs, or with friends and family, we may be pillars of confidence and strength. But in the world of romantic love and relationship, we are just bundles of nerves. Sometimes just the thought of making an emotional connection is enough to set us on edge; we are anxious before we begin. We "enter twitching," and we continue twitching as the connection deepens and we feel even more vulnerable. Sometimes the anxiety is minimal; sometimes it's overwhelming.

Here's a partial list of some of the things about love that make us anxious:

We fear rejection. We fear comparison. We fear loss. We fear abandonment. We fear being revealed. And we fear losing our freedom and independence. We fear losing too much sleep. We fear losing our favorite closet. We fear expectations. We fear engulfment. We fear that our physical and intellectual limitations will be exposed—and judged. We fear disappointment. We fear new priorities. We fear increased responsibility. We fear our own vulnerability. And we fear our own intense feelings. We fear losing control. We fear heartbreak. We fear making another mistake. We fear that this person might represent our last chance at finding love. We fear being misunderstood. We fear not being appreciated. We fear being taken for granted. And we fear we can't deliver the goods. We fear repeating the past. We fear that the past will haunt us. We fear that the future will disappoint us. We fear sex—particularly monogamous sex and it's implications. We fear "going too far." We fear not going far enough. We fear the many ghosts that surface to remind us of how difficult relationships are.

And, most important, we fear the feelings associated with anxiety itself.

What We Do With Our Anxieties

Anxiety is a difficult emotion. When we feel anxious, our stomachs hurt, our chests ache, our hearts beat faster. Anxiety scares us; it overwhelms us; it keeps us off balance. It distracts us and keeps us from concentrating on our work. It's downright painful. IT CAN KEEP US FROM ENJOYING LIFE ITSELF.

Small wonder that we'll do almost anything to get rid of that feeling. But what can we do? In relationships, we typically try to control our anxieties by trying to control how much we feel or don't feel. We also try to control what our partners do or don't do, and we try to control the outcome of the relationship itself.

In our heart of hearts, we all know that relationships should evolve gradually and naturally. Our anxieties, however, often make us want to short circuit that process. We want to know that we have options; we want to know that we have some kind of control. That need to control our anxieties makes us do dumb stuff. Sometimes it makes us push our partners away. Sometimes it makes us try to pull our partners closer. Sometimes it makes us start fights; sometimes it makes us want to throw up.

Naming Our Anxieties

Often just acknowledging and naming our anxieties helps us get a handle on understanding how they can sabotage our connections. Here are some of the ways our anxieties make us act out and, consequently, stand in the way of commitment.

Bailing out the Moment We Feel Panic (Instead of Learning to Understand and Work With Our Fears)

If performers left the stage the moment they felt anxious, we would have no opera, dance, or theatre. If athletes returned to the locker room whenever they felt anxious, we would have no sports to speak of. If businessmen walked out of their meetings at the first sign of anxiety, our economy would grind to a halt. If public speakers left the podium the second they got anxious, we would never have to listen to another speech. And if each of us bailed from our relationships the moment we got anxious, there would be no relationships left standing. Anxiety is not necessarily a *bad* thing. It is just a challenging thing. And you need to rise and meet the challenge.

Ask any couple whose relationship you truly respect, and they will probably tell you the same thing: when a relationship is in its beginnings—even the *best* relationship—there will be many times when you feel uncertain, doubtful, or even totally panic-stricken. "Is this right?" "Is the timing right?" "Is this the one" "Am I really ready for this?"

All of these questions have good answers. But here's the problem: they don't have good answers *now*. Which is why it is such a mistake to *do* anything *now*, except take a lot of deep breaths and "ride the wave." You have to learn to work internally with your fear, instead of letting your fear call all the shots. You have to find an "adult" voice inside of you that can keep your fear in its place until you clearly understand its origins, or until it eventually subsides.

Anxiety may be evidence that you and your partner are moving closer. See this as a *positive* sign.

The answers to your anxious questions will present themselves over time as a relationship runs its course. Right now, only one thing is certain: bailing out is not the answer. Give the relationship a chance. What seems so scary today may seem foolish or irrelevant tomorrow. It may feel manageable tomorrow. It may *disappear* tomorrow, leaving you to wonder "what was that all about?" Your job is to get to tomorrow, instead of folding before you even look at all your cards.

Getting Turned on by Your Partner's Loss (or Lack) of Interest

If you had asked Bryce four days ago how he felt about Melissa, the woman he was dating, he would have told you that he thought "she was okay." But if you ask him how he's feeling today, he will tell you he thinks he's in love with her. What happened to create such a sudden change of heart? Melissa just told Bryce she doesn't want to date him exclusively.

If you had asked Jennifer two weeks ago what she felt about the long-term prospects of her relationship with Keith, she would have told you she's not really sure he's "the one." But if you ask her today, she will tell you that she would marry him right now if he asked her. What happened to create such a sudden shift? Yesterday Keith told Jennifer he's not sure she's "the one" for him.

Here's the ultimate knee-jerk response for people who struggle with commitment fears: suddenly getting more interested the moment your partner becomes less interested. If you inevitably change your position and suddenly want "in" the moment you start to suspect your partner wants "out," you have to realize that this is a reaction that has little to do with genuine feelings or honest motivation.

You need to get a grip on this one because it's a symptom of not wanting a relationship that has the potential to work. Try to understand how someone else's disinterest leaves you free to fantasize, yearn, and even act without having to consider any consequences. For a relationship to work, both partners have to want the same thing at the same time. If you don't have that in common, it doesn't matter what else you have in common.

Putting Too Much Pressure Too Soon

A lot of people want to get the dating/relationship-building thing out of the way as quickly as possible so they can alleviate their anxiety and "return to their normal lives." Maybe this is how you feel, and it's why you're in such a rush. Or maybe you're afraid your feelings will change if you wait much longer, or that your partner's feelings will change. Or maybe this is your way of intentionally scaring off solid prospects. Whatever your reasons, your timing is scary, and it makes you appear to lack a clear sense of appropriate relationship development. Your prospective partner can't help but wonder, "Who is he/she having this relationship with?... It certainly isn't with me."

The early stages of a relationship give both partners an invaluable opportunity for exploration. It is a time to make mistakes and learn from those mistakes, and a time to gather necessary information that will help you make grounded, integrated decisions about the long-term potential of the relationship. These beginnings, though they may be filled with anxiety and pressure, are part of the relationship process. Trying to shorten the process only adds another dimension of anxiety and pressure to the picture, seriously challenging your chances for success.

Rejecting in Order to Avoid Being Rejected

Charles really loves Selma, but he's feeling enormous pressure, not only from her, but also from work. He just told Selma that he wants to see less of her for the next few weeks because he has to get a big project done at work. How did Selma respond? By telling him that if he feels that way maybe they should stop seeing each other. Period.

In this case, Charles really does just want a little bit of time and distance in order to catch up on office work and evaluate the relationship. If Selma had responded by asking Charles to define what he meant, it might have provided an opportunity for both partners to articulate their feelings, and hence helped their relationship to grow. If her attitude conveyed that she understood and she too needed some free time, it would have opened up possibilities for both partners. As it is, Selma's reaction didn't help the relationship. Charles doesn't want to lose Selma, so he smoothed over her feelings and stopped talking about time off. However, he is feeling enormously resentful and angry. He doesn't want to go through life feeling this way, which is making him seriously question this relationship.

We've all experienced this scenario: You are convinced that the axe is about to fall, so you grab your own axe and take the first swing. For a little while it makes you feel better; it makes you feel empowered. But then you start to wonder if you acted too quickly and harshly. Problem is, you'll never know.

Many times, that "certain" feeling that rejection is imminent is a projection we are struggling with from the past. Something about our partner's words or behavior is too reminiscent of a past partner's words or behavior, and we immediately jump to a negative conclusion. But the assumptions we make can be completely off.

Some people fight as a prelude to breaking off their relationships, but some people fight just to let off steam. Some people say they "need their space" as an excuse to end a relationship, and some people say they "need their space" because they just need a day or two to themselves. Some people don't return a phone call because they're trying to get out of a relationship, but some people don't return a phone call because they're overwhelmed that day. There is only one way to tell the difference: you need more information. I am not suggesting you stay involved and vulnerable in a relationship that is clearly doing you harm. I am only suggesting that you have good, clear information, and that you are feeling balanced and clear before you make any decisions that are firm and final.

Controlling in Order to Avoid "Space Invasion" and Other Anxiety-Provoking Situations

A relationship requires compromise. That means that you're not going to get your own way about every little thing. For some people that feels as though they are losing their freedom and control of their own environment. That produces anxiety. Often we respond by trying to control even more.

I, for example, know that I sometimes try to control my anxieties by controlling my partner's behavior. Who doesn't? As a single person, I became very accustomed to controlling my own environment. Then as my various relationships would get more intimate, I would regularly face my control issues. Often this would reveal itself around the issues of space. I would feel my space being taken over; it would make me anxious; I would try to take control of what was happening.

Whenever a woman began to spend time in my "space" (my one-bedroom bachelor apartment), I would soon start to feel as though I was losing control of my apartment, and I didn't like it. A part of me would turn into a caricature of an inflexible, fussy bachelor. And even if I didn't share this with the woman, I reacted internally. "Her" stuff would be all over the bathroom, kitchen, and living room. "She" would start moving things. In the refrigerator, the mustard would end up behind the orange juice instead of the other way around. It felt like a "space" invasion. The milk would get finished (how could anyone drink so much milk?), and no more milk would be purchased. I knew exactly when it was time to buy more milk from the weight of the carton in my hand when I picked it up. But when a woman began spending time in my apartment, a new factor would appear: *someone else drinking my milk.* You can see that I would have some pretty obnoxious thoughts. Without being aware that I was experiencing relationship anxiety, I would blame my partner.

I remember thinking that I needed things neat, and this other person was creating chaos. I couldn't handle stepping over someone else's things, for example. I tell you this just so you can get some idea of how silly the reasoning of someone with commitment conflicts can get. When I would begin to feel that my someone else was impinging on my space, I would sometimes focus on toilet paper. Incredibly stupid, I know. But I couldn't handle someone else using so much more toilet paper than I do.

In what I thought of as my perfect state of singular aloneness, I used to calculate precisely how many rolls of toilet paper I needed for three months and have them stored in a closet. "*She*, whoever she might be," what with makeup and everything, would sometimes go through my three-month acquisition in a couple of weeks. It made me feel angry. I accept the fact that my unrecognized anxiety made me generally impossible and controlling about all kinds of stupid little stuff.

Setting up house with my wife brought me into many of the same issues, all having to do with control. Jill, for example, immediately wanted to "doll up" our spare bedroom for houseguests. I didn't want to spend the money and felt it wasn't a priority. I thought guests should be happy just to have a room of their own. "Why not?" I reasoned with what seemed to me to be perfect logic. But Jill wanted not just a room, but a *nice* room. She started buying furniture, some of which she acknowledged was temporary at best. Suddenly I felt as though my immediate environment was getting out of control. I found it emotionally disruptive because I find interim solutions anxiety provoking.

We've certainly had our arguments over these issues. Even when I disagree vehemently with what Jill is doing, I can see that it wouldn't be nearly as big a problem if I didn't have such a need to control my immediate space. And, of course, I would like to have more control over Jill's choices.

In the "pink" period of a new relationship, it feels as though it doesn't really matter what you do or don't do with space. It doesn't matter if bags are left on the floor, clothes are left lying around, beds are made or unmade, the stereo is on or off, the windows are open or closed. But, as the relationship gets real, these issues can become major; for many people, it can feel like a life or death battle. You need to remember that the issue is the anxiety you are feeling about losing control of the environment. Your arguments are not about values, or styles, or hygiene. They are about control—control of your environment and the other person's behavior.

We all suffer from some frustration that our partners are different than we are and that we can't control their likes, dislikes, needs, or style of behavior. My wife adjusts to these issues faster than I do. I admit, I find them difficult. However, I have learned to recognize what is happening, and it makes a big difference. It can make a difference in your relationships too.

Control and connection are like water and oil. They simply do not mix. Genuine intimate connection can only occur in the absence of control, when both partners fully "let go." Relationship is all about risk, and control is the opposite of risk. Control gets in the way of feelings. Control is manipulation, and it closes the chambers of the heart.

Having More Intense Relationships With Our Anxiety Than We Do With Our Partners

We all have anxiety buttons. Push the right buttons, and just about anyone will go into a discombobulating spin. Some of us spin more often and more frequently. But why do so many of us end up with partners who know just when and how to push our anxiety buttons? Which comes first? Are we responding first to partners because they know which buttons to push? Or are we inadvertently responding first to the anxiety buttons themselves?

In relationships, these are very important questions. Here's why. Often we end up feeling strongly about someone simply because we believe this person has the power to set and reset our anxiety buttons. He or she tripped the switch that gave us the initial anxiety attack. Perhaps he/she was unfaithful, unpredictable, or rejective. We become so anxious that we therefore believe resolving things with this partner is the only way our anxiety can be relieved.

Here's something else that often happens: The relationship feels so bonded and the attraction is so strong that it brings up all sorts of buried feelings from our personal history. We become anxious—so anxious in fact that the only way we believe we can get relief is to get away from the relationship and the partner who evokes these feelings.

Feelings of anxiety can be provoked by a fear of loss and deconnection; they can also be provoked by strong positive connections. What we have to do is realize that these are anxieties that we carry with us. They can, and will, be provoked in any number of situations. It's up to each of us individually to get a handle on how and why we become anxious. When we do this, (a) we won't find ourselves feeling victimized by partners who control us by controlling our anxieties; and (b) we won't find ourselves running away from potentially wonderful partners who have inadvertently stirred some internal anxiety stew.

SOME ESSENTIAL TIPS FOR HANDLING RELATIONSHIP ANXIETY

Learn How to Deconstruct Your Anxiety

Anxiety doesn't appear out of nowhere, and it doesn't necessarily come from only one source. In order to get a handle on what's happening, you need to be able to put your anxiety in a centrifuge and spin it until you can clearly see the complex composition. In this way you can work with each piece separately. In short, take your anxiety apart:

- Here's the piece where he/she reminds me of my little brother/sister who used to take all my toys and break them, and I feel as though I will spend my whole life stuck with someone who is taking advantage of me.
- Here's the piece where he/she taps into all my image issues and makes me anxious that I will always be with someone who makes me worried about what others will think.
- Here's the piece where he/she pushes all of my insecurity buttons, and makes me worry about being abandoned and lonely forever.

When we are upset, our anxieties and our need to feel in control get all mixed up together. Combine that with the way you choose to get that control back (create distance, move away, pick a fight, pick apart), and it becomes one big jumble. It's an illusion that all of these components create one hopeless mess. Once you have all the pieces on the table in front of you, you will see that you can work with each one of them separately.

Don't Escalate Your Anxiety by Practicing "Either...Or" Thinking

For example: Vinnie and Cheri have an ongoing disagreement about Cheri's brother, Ray, and Ray's best friend, Donny. Vinnie is jealous because he feels Cheri spends too much time on the phone with both of them. He feels Cheri, Ray, and Donny are much *too* close and he can't handle it. Cheri says Vinnie is wrong because the three of them grew up together and are like siblings. Cheri says that Ray and Donny like to talk to her about their problems with girlfriends; Cheri likes to listen. Vinnie says that he believes that Donny is romantically interested in Cheri and that Ray is supporting his interest.

Last week Vinnie issued an ultimatum: "Either you stop hanging out with those two guys, or the relationship is over!" Cheri said that she doesn't intend to spend the rest of her life with someone who is policing her behavior. In this argument, Vinnie and Cheri got very close to the edge. Both said things they wished they hadn't said. They managed to smooth over the conflict...temporarily. But it hasn't gone away and it hasn't been resolved. In this argument, we can see that both Vinnie and Cheri are getting too close to "either...or" thinking.

In truth, Vinnie doesn't have enough information to know whether his suspicions about Donny are realistic. And he certainly doesn't have the right to ask Cheri not to talk to her brother. Cheri also doesn't really know whether Vinnie's jealousy is so extreme that he's not going to make a good partner. Instead of letting their separate anxieties take them in separate directions, Vinnie and Cheri need to find a way to work with the relationship. Can the situation be defused? Can Cheri see a little less of Ray and Donny? Can Vinnie agree to be friendly and to go to a movie or out for a pizza with the three of them so that he can become more comfortable with their friendship?

Sometimes when we are anxious, we become so uncomfortable about what we fear that we "just want to get it over with." So we push the situation even further. "If it's going to end, let it end now," becomes our operating mantra. And often our insistence that "either it's 100 percent perfect (which of course nothing is), or it's nothing" attitude gets the result we fear most: A relationship in shambles.

Learn How to Breathe Through Your Fear

• Your partner isn't responding with as much passion or intensity as he/she usually does. You panic. Is he/she still attracted to me? Is he/she drifting away? You have a whole arsenal of emotional ploys you can use to rev up the relationship and get the emotional feedback you need to feed your insecurities: You can start a fight; you can cry; you can demand explanations.

- He/she is five minutes late getting ready. You suddenly imagine a lifetime of waiting. It makes you feel anxious and trapped. You're ready to start a major argument and walk out the door.
- He/she has chosen to buy a car you hate in a color you despise. You become anxious about what people will think of you driving around in such a stupid vehicle. This, you think, looking at the partner you truly adore, is more than even I can take. You're ready to start a domestic war.

Counting to ten is a first step in emergencies. Take it a step further. Learn to breathe through your fear. This is the now-walk-away-from-the-gun phase of violent crime management. Take it from one who is fully versed in the art of relationship sabatoge: There were many times in the beginning of my relationship with my wife that the only thing that stopped me from sabotaging connection was just long slow breaths and waiting until my immediate anxiety-induced reactions passed. And they would pass.

I used to make fun of people who talked about the power of breath, but I learned how to use breath to move me through my anxieties. When we are terrified, we tend to hold our breath in until it demands relief—expanding to explosive or paralyzing proportions. So all together now, breathe in the good air, breathe out the fear.

Don't Escalate Your Anxiety by Obsessing About Your Anxiety

The relationship you have with your anxiety can begin to resemble the engine of a locomotive. Once a fire has started, you begin to shovel in the coal faster and faster until you've created the roaring fire from hell.

For example: Martha and Syd have been going out for a couple of months. This week Syd said his parents were having some problems, and he had to go back home for the weekend. He didn't call Martha all weekend, and it's now Monday morning, and there has been no phone call. Martha remembers her last boyfriend, Sean, who used to do this kind of thing regularly. She is becoming hysterical. She calls her best friend. She calls Syd. The machine answers. She hangs up. She repeats this process several times. She calls her best friend again. Together they imagine likely scenarios. All of them feature a Syd who is either cheating or lying in a ditch somewhere, crying Martha's name.

Martha begins to wonder whether Syd has been having an affair with the woman who was flirting with him in his building elevator. Yes, she thinks. That's it! She calls her best friend again. They discuss this possibility.

Who knows where Syd is? But Martha will find out soon enough. Why can't she let it go? It's always a mistake to let your anxiety consume you until it is all you can feel. YOU HAVE A CHOICE: You can take your anxiety outside until it passes, or you can take it to critical mass.

Don't Let Your Behavior Mirror Your Conflict

Sometimes conflicted emotions get acted out in contradictory ways. One moment you are craving your own space, then two days later you are asking your partner to go with you to Hawaii. Try to imagine how confusing and hurtful it must be for your partner to have his/her life turned upside down, right side up, and shaken from side to side by your behavioral swings.

When you are caught up in the swings of your commitment conflict, it's very easy to act out those swings in very large ways—breaking up, making up, moving out, moving back in, heavy fighting, and heavier apologizing. This back-and-forthing is one of the most destructive things that people with active commitment conflicts do. So keep this in mind, and try to do your testing and sorting by yourself, with a trusted but unbiased friend or family member who can keep your feelings confidential forever, or in the office of a skilled professional. Just remember to let any actions you take in the relationship reflect well-thought-out decisions, not your work in progress.

Recognize Your Anxious Fight-or-Flight Reaction for What It Is

Many people have been so sensitized by their personal emotional history, that the moment they become close to another human being, they experience feelings associated with people suffering from phobias. These classic phobic responses include waves of anxiety, a sense of dread, hyperventilation and/or labored breathing, suffocating sensations, skipping or racing hearts, stomach distress, excessive sweating, or even chills. We can experience these feelings whenever we become afraid. Sometimes we are afraid of experiencing feelings of loss (similar to ones we may have already experienced in our personal history); sometimes we associate unpleasant emotions with intimate relationships, and we become afraid of these; sometimes the closeness of an intimate relationship makes us feel genuinely claustrophobic.

back-and-forthing is one of the most destructive things people with active commitment conflicts do

You can't handle your anxiety if you don't recognize it when it's staring you in the face. For example:

When Liam isn't in a relationship, he's a relatively passive guy who spends too much time alone. However, the minute one of his relationships starts to get serious, he suddenly becomes aware of all the various women he wants to have sex with before he settles down. This is the "flight" part of a fight-or-flight response.

When Max and Brittany first met, Max thought Brittany was incredibly smart and good looking. Now that the relationship is deepening, Max is starting to see Brittany's imperfections. And, as he sees them, he brings them to Brittany's attention. One by one. In a condescending tone. "Why can't you use larger bags for the garbage pail so the bags wouldn't be so difficult to secure?" "How could you forget to recycle that large plastic soda bottle?" When she made that six-course romantic dinner for the two of them followed by a night of passionate sex, "Why didn't you remember to put soap suds in the pot you cooked the chicken in overnight? Now the kitchen sink is greasy, and it doesn't look particularly hygenic. I can't stand looking at it." Watching Max find fault with Brittany provides a perfect lesson in relationship sabotage. This is the "fight" part of a fight-or-flight response.

As a connection deepens, and qualms, doubts, and fears arise, we need to recognize anxiety for what it is. We need to recognize when anxiety is the reason why we want to fight, act out, run away, or cheat. The next time you have a destructive impulse in your relationship, try to stop and imagine what is driving that impulse. What is providing all that energy? There is a very good chance that it is your anxieties that are out of control.

See Anxiety As an Emotion, Not a Mandate

Some people don't recognize anxiety as an emotion that will pass with time. For example:

Clint is thinking about moving in with Winnie, but it's making him nervous. Standing in line at a supermarket he's beginning to feel really anxious. Can he do this? Will he be happy? Maybe he really wants to date other people. He sees a pretty blonde with a grocery cart stacked high with tofu and veggies. He starts a conversation. Faster than you can say stir-fry, he gets her phone number. As he does this, he begins to feel less anxious about moving in with Winnie. But he has new issues about which to get anxious. Suppose he asks out the pretty blonde vegetarian? Suppose Winnie finds out? Even more anxiety.

Some people still don't see anxiety as an emotion. Instead they see it as a mandate to take action. They don't always know they are anxious; they only know that "something is wrong." They feel unhappy. They may have stomach upsets, headaches, palpitations, or a pervasive sense of dread; they may even feel weak in the knees. Typically, instead of sitting with the discomfort and figuring it out, we tend to want to run away from both the feeling and the person whom we blame for inducing the feeling—*i.e.,* our significant other. We want to do something—anything—to get away from the way we feel when we are anxious. Often the things we do trying to escape anxiety creates even more problems and more anxiety.

Anxiety, like any other emotion, can't control you unless you let it. You have a choice. Relationship anxiety is simply an emotional response to a situation that is inherently scary: Getting genuinely close to another human being. Don't assume that your anxiety is a "sign" that you are making a mistake.

Find a Pace You Can Live With, Not a Pace That Sets You on Edge

You know yourself. You know what makes you become so involved that your anxieties become stirred up. What makes you get anxious about losing what you have? What makes you feel as though you are in over your head? When we begin new relationships, too often we either rush forward—or allow ourselves to be rushed forward. It all becomes too important, too soon. Don't expect the moon and the stars, and you won't be so much on edge. Always hold back a little bit for yourself so that you don't become overwhelmed by your anxious tendencies.

Whenever we create situations that fill us or our partners with anxiety, we are being our own worst enemies. Certain things move a relationship forward very quickly, so be careful with those things. Don't use sex to move a relationship forward. Don't make plans for the future before the relationship is ready. That includes vacation and holiday plans as well as plans to get engaged or married or move in together.

It's true that in a relationship at least part of the anxiety comes in reaction to things happening outside of you, but much of your anxiety can also be of your own creation. You set a pace, and it fries you;

you make promises, and your own promises horrify you; you comply with your own fantasies of how a relationship is supposed to evolve, and it puts you in a pressure cooker of your own making.

Find a *You* You Can Live With

- Paul thinks that Randall expects him to dress and act the part of a successful book editor, so he complies by wearing flannel jackets and going to poetry readings even though he would rather wear sweats and hang out on city basketball courts.
- Dodi is a few years older than Geoff. She's so worried about looking older that she takes six exercise classes a week and never hangs out with people her own age.

Anxiety is created whenever you try to be someone other than the full person you really are, and then try to live up to that false persona. Whether you like it or not, the real you is the only person who can handle a real relationship. And, as I've probably said before, if your relationship doesn't work out, you want to know that it didn't work out for *you*, not because you *hid* the real you.

Build a Life That's Strong Enough to Withstand Anxious Winds

- Loretta believes that she can't live without love. She is certain that if her relationship with Josh ends, she will barely be able to breathe.
- Woody has wrapped all his dreams and hopes around his life with Deedee. What will he do if she disappoints him?

We become more or less anxious depending on the height of the stakes. For some people, having a relationship consumes their lives. They want it so much. Perhaps too much. Small wonder they are always filled with relationship anxiety.

As children we all learned the lesson of the three little pigs. Remember the cute little pig who was smart enough to build a house of bricks. The smart little pig's house was so strong that not even the big bad wolf could blow it down. Build a life that gives you so much pleasure that you worry whether you will ever be able to change it—even for the love of your life.

The more "life" you have balancing you, the less likely you are to suffer from acute relationship anxiety. While there is still much to gain from having love in your life, there is less to lose if, for any reason, it doesn't work out.

Figure Out the Difference Between a Partner Who Is Making You Anxious and the Anxiety That You Bring to the Table

Let's face it, some people work at making their partners anxious. If you are with someone who is lying, cheating, or manipulating, he or she is creating your anxiety. Ditto a partner who doesn't call or show up when he/she is supposed to; a partner who has a thousand stories that sound fishy; a partner who withholds love or sets unreasonable boundaries; or a partner who is trying to control your behavior or unreasonably pressuring you for more closeness than you want. This is a partner who is actively sabotaging the relationship. There are valid reasons why you are becoming anxious. What you have to ask yourself is why you are *staying* anxious. It's up to you to take steps to get counseling or end the relationship.

Get some immediate insight to help you figure out who or what is creating your anxiety. Remember, crisis counseling starts by opening a dialogue with yourself. Talk the problem through—out loud. Welcome all the different voices that are contributing to your discomfort. Write down your feelings and what is taking place. This is for you. It's a step to help you. Don't use what you have written down as a way of obsessing over the many ways your partner may have hurt you. What you are doing is trying to take appropriate action for yourself.

Remember that even if your partner is "trying" to make you anxious, if you're not carrying around easily accessed anxieties, you won't respond so predictably.

Get in Touch With Your "Regulator"

Gena, a single mother, and Dean have been dating each other for a couple of months, going out approximately once every two weeks. They first had sex last weekend. At the time Dean suggested that perhaps he and Gena could go away for a long weekend. Gena took him very literally and started arranging for a babysitter. After he made the suggestion, Dean had second thoughts—most of them financial. He doesn't have the money to go away right now.

Today over dinner, Gena started to talk about their planned weekend, and Dean had to tell her that he didn't know if he could do it. Gena's immediate reaction—disappointment—quickly switched to anxiety (what was Dean really saying?). Then, trying to overcome her feelings, Gena became defensive and angry. Where, she asked, did Dean think the relationship was headed? Dean said, "Well, I don't know. I thought we enjoyed each other's company. I thought we would date and see what happened." Gena responded by saying, "I've heard this before. I know exactly where this is going. I have a daughter who I have to protect here. I think it's better just to end it right now." And she stormed out of the restaurant. Basically, Gena flipped. She took this as an opportunity to voluntarily lose herself in her own dreaded scenarios.

When Gena confronted Dean, there was no "regulator" at work. There was no third party giving advice, no forum for addressing the problem, no nothing. Gena's instincts were right on one level. If she was feeling so bad about what Dean said, those feelings needed to be addressed. But how? As she began to feel anxious about her future with Dean, Gena needed to take a minute to figure out how. She needed to get in touch with her own internal regulator. Gena could have taken the issue home with her so she could rationally decide what, if anything, should be done or said. She could have taken a day or two to cool down—or a week for that matter. She could have gone home, taken a nice bath, had a glass of warm milk, and gone to bed, trying to get a good night's sleep with the hope that it would all look different in the morning. Or, sitting in the restaurant, she could have had a real conversation with Dean about what it all meant and what everyone was feeling. But Gena didn't even count to ten. If she had she might have left room for her internal "regulator" to take control and find balance in the situation.

Gena allowed everything to escalate in her mind to the worst possible place, the place where she became so frightened of her anxious feelings that she experienced the classic phobic symptoms—fight-or-flight. And she embraced both of these feelings. Many people are like Gena. When the relationship looks as though it might have any element of disappointment, they find it easier to let it all get out of control and then end it. That way you don't have to live through the reality of the relationship and see whether or not it is a relationship that can bend and adjust to fit both partners, which is what a real relationship will do.

Let's suppose Gena handled this differently. Let's suppose Gena simply said:

"Oh, that makes me so disappointed. I was looking forward to spending time with you alone."

Gena was genuinely upset. What made her think it was better to have Dean see her anger than her disappointment? After all, this is what she was authentically feeling. How might Dean have responded to her disappointment? Gena would have learned a great deal about the future of the relationship from that response. Dean might have found it endearing. He might have discussed his own feelings of disappointment as well as his own problems. This could have been a growth moment for the relationship. Instead it turned into a showdown.

Whenever you experience anxious fight-or-flight reactions, you need to get in touch with your regulator before doing anything.

Consider Talking to a Professional About Your Anxiety

I can't say enough about the pivotal role good help can play in helping you handle relationship anxiety. A good therapist should be able to help you examine your life so you can get to the place where your core anxieties are being generated. A good therapist should be able to help you evaluate your relationship realistically. A good therapist should be able to help you access your "regulator." When you seek counseling, you're taking care of yourself. Don't let your anxieties make you walk away from good relationships; don't let your anxieties keep you from ending those that need ending.

Hang On!

Living through relationship anxiety is like riding a wild horse. Truly. If you hang on and stay in control, the horse *will* get tired. Knowing that the horse will eventually get tired also makes it more motivating to try to survive the ride. You are stronger than your anxieties. You are. You can make a commitment to yourself; you can stop being driven by anxiety, whether that anxiety is caused by a fear of loss or a fear of commitment. And you can make an appropriate commitment to another human being without being overwhelmed by anxiety and fear.

Your anxiety has many things to teach you if you let it. Try to think of anxiety as an instructor trying to lead you to information. This information is very valuable. You need it for your relationships and you need it for your own growth in general. If you fly off the handle or out of your relationships to get away from your anxiety, you are throwing out the baby, the bathwater, and the tub.

CONCLUSION

Getting What You Want

When I first decided to write this book, I wanted it to be short and sweet: "Out with the old, in with the new, by following a few easy steps...." And I wanted it to have a very positive, hopeful message because I feel very positive and hopeful about the future of relationships. Then the writing began, and I was quickly reminded how complex and multi-layered the issue of commitment continues to be.

While I would like to think of the process of "getting to commitment" as a celebration of the possibility for lasting love, I know more than anything this has been a book about cleaning house. Old choices, old habits, old fantasies, old programs, old language, old doubts, and old fears. All of this has to be boxed, sealed, and moved out of your path to clear the way to commitment. But once you move the worst stuff out of your way, or at least put it into clearer perspective, something extraordinary starts to happen. There is healing, there is understanding, there is forgiveness, there is emotional reorganization. The possibility for real love and commitment slowly blossoms in front of you like a beautiful flower. Something that has seemed so complicated suddenly seems so simple, straightforward, and clear. Something that has seemed so foreign suddenly feels so natural and right.

It's a lot like tennis, if I may make an analogy. It takes hundreds of lessons and thousands of hours of practice and uncountable numbers of hit tennis balls to make it look easy and feel easy. Once you have that, it feels like the most natural thing in the world, and you can't remember what a struggle it was to reach that point. Today my wife comes home, kisses me hello at the door, and it feels like the most natural thing in the world. But getting to this point took hard work.

Right now, you may be wondering, "How long will it take to bring commitment into my life?" "How will I know if I'm doing the right thing?" "How do I know if I'm ready?" "Can I meet the challenges presented by this relationship?" "Is it worth the struggle?" I obviously cannot answer all your questions individually with complete prescience, but I can leave you with a short set of rules I hope you will live by on your unique and challenging journey to a committed relationship.

Getting to Commitment . . . TAKES DESIRE

You have to really want this in your life. Otherwise it won't feel as though it is worth the work, and you will always be looking for opportunities and reasons to quit. This isn't something you should be doing because people tell you that you have a problem. Or because you feel guilty. This is something you should be doing because you are clear about what commitment means and why you want it in your life.

Getting to Commitment . . . TAKES TIME

The relationship you want isn't going to happen over night just because you feel that you are "ready." Commitment is a process that develops slowly, in stages, and is always evolving. Your anxiety to have something meaningful won't accelerate the process. It just doesn't work that way. If anything, it can work against you. Think of this as though you are building a house you want to live in and you are doing it piece by piece, which is the only way such a house can be built. Let yourself enjoy the construction process.

Getting to Commitment . . . TAKES ENERGY

It doesn't matter how terrific your partner is, and it doesn't matter how intense the chemistry. A committed relationship is always going to be hard work. But it is the work that brings love into your life, and that is an extraordinary reward.

Getting to Commitment . . . TAKES RISK

You will have to take chances. You will have to be vulnerable. You will have to truly open your heart. When it comes to building a loving, committed relationship, there is no way to play it safe. The only way you can protect yourself is by playing it SLOW, something I always encourage doing. If this is the relationship of the century, you will have a century to enjoy it. So take your risks in small manageable increments.

Getting to Commitment . . . TAKES HELP

Getting ready to spend the rest of your life with another human being is something you don't have to do by yourself. I don't even think you should *try* to do it by yourself. Support is available from so many places if you ask. Friends and family can give you great strength if you make your desires clear. Support groups like CODA (Codependents Anonymous) and ACA (Adult Children of Alcoholics) can give you great strength. Spiritual and church groups can also help. And don't forget about professional help from trained counselors and therapists. A little counseling can go a long way in helping a couple survive the getting-to-know-you phase of a relationship.

Getting to Commitment . . . TAKES TWO

Please, please remember that a committed relationship is only possible when both partners are striving for the same thing, at the same time. Your desire is critical, but so is the desire of your partner. Being completely committed to an uncommitted partner is an exercise in futility, and often a disguise for your own unexplored fears. If you and your partner are not working toward the same goal, then it's unlikely that your hard work will be rewarded.

Getting to Commitment . . . TAKES FAITH

You have to believe that a real loving connection with another human being is possible. Regardless of your relationship history, regardless of your family history, and in spite of your fears, you have to have faith. Yes, it can be difficult; yes, it can feel overwhelming. But know from your heart that love is within your reach. I know from years of experience that this is possible for you. But you have to bring your own faith to the table.

Real commitment is magical. It will transform you. Making a life with someone you love who loves you back can only bring out the best in you. The wonderful thing about commitment—the truly amazing thing—is that it gives back so much more than it takes.

Getting Beyond the Eight Greatest Obstacles to Love— A Brief Review

Challenge One: The Courage to Stop Blaming

Blame masks the truth; it always leads to feelings of alienation and separateness. Blame stops you from ever learning anything valuable from the relationships that have failed you. Every relationship has two responsible parties. As long as you blame other people's shortcomings or struggles for the lack of commitment in your life, you will not move forward and you will not grow. Change begins when you take responsibility for your feelings and your fears, your successes and your failures.

Challenge Two: The Courage to Say Goodbye to Your Ghosts

All of us are haunted by our history. All of us carry complex baggage. Study your past. Embrace it in order to heal it. And let yourself learn from it. Let yourself learn how your history controls your choices and your behavior. Let yourself learn how your ghosts are responsible for your complex emotions. Change begins when you face your history.

Challenge Three: The Courage to Find and Fight for the Self

Learning more about who you are, accepting who you are, and standing up for who you are is part of the process of being in a relationship. Until you begin paying attention to your lack of self-awareness, lack of self-respect, lack of self-care, and lack of self-love, you will not move forward. Change begins when the relationship you have with yourself is one you truly value, and one you can share with another human being.

Challenge Four: The Courage to Stay Grounded in Reality

Real life and real love happen in a real relationship with a real partner in the real world. A life led in fantasy (whether the fantasy is yours or someone else's) may bring magical experiences of love, but it doesn't lead to a love you can trust. For that, you must stay real and grounded. This may sound boring if you have never done it, but it doesn't feel boring when you are in it because it is so alive and meaningful. Change begins when your feet touch the floor, and you are willing to keep that connection.

Challenge Five: The Courage to Allow Yourself to Be Known

Making a loving connection that "sticks" and strengthens over time requires revealing your genuine self, piece by piece. It means wisely sharing your thoughts and feelings about your history as well as new experiences. If you stay hidden in your relationships, you deny yourself and your partner the glue that will keep you together. If you are hoping that physical intimacy alone will create a lasting bond, you are short-changing your relationship of much of its richness. Change begins when you become visible.

Challenge Six: The Courage to Learn the Lessons of Acceptance

Come to terms with image issues that lead you to destructive choices. Stop being critical and non-accepting of potentially loving partners and open the door to human connection. Letting yourself be controlled by your desire to find perfection keeps you disconnected and empty. If you are holding on to primitive idealizations of what your partner should look like, sound like, or act like, you will not move forward. Change begins when you acknowledge and accept "humanness" in yourself and others.

Challenge Seven: The Courage to Define a New Path

The old path will continue to lead you back to square one. Your old patterns are not going to change by themselves, and they will not change just because you wish for something different. Creating change requires shedding the old habits that keep you stuck in self-defeating circumstances. It requires taking steps in new directions. Stop waiting for a different kind of partner to bring out a better you—a different kind of you. Change begins when you decide that *you* are capable of acting differently in relationships and capable of building a relationship that will last.

Challenge Eight: The Courage to Handle Your Anxieties

Don't give in to your fear of intimacy. Becoming more powerful in the face of your fear is within your grasp. Anxiety is part and parcel of the connection process. Getting close enough to create a lasting bond will always bring questions and ambivalence. Vulnerability is a constant. Self-doubts surface regularly. As a relationship deepens, the perceived loss of freedom can sometimes feel overwhelming. Expect some anxieties to surface. All of this is normal. Perhaps even more important, all of this is very survivable if you stop running away. If you let the fear take over, you won't move forward. Change begins when you assure yourself that you are bigger than your fear.